SUCCESSFUL ICT LEADERSHIP
IN PRIMARY SCHOOLS

John College
entre

22 MAY 2022

I0582347

3 8025 00457539 8

Successful ICT Leadership
in Primary Schools

Bob Fox

YORK ST. JOHN
COLLEGE LIBRARY

Learning Matters

First published in 2003 by Learning Matters Ltd.

All rights reserved. No part of this publication may be reproduced, stored in a retrieval system, or transmitted in any form or by any means, electronic, mechanical, photocopying, recording, or otherwise, without prior permission in writing from Learning Matters.

© 2003 Bob Fox

British Library Cataloguing in Publication Data
A CIP record for this book is available from the British Library.

ISBN 1 903300 80 0

Cover design by Topics – The Creative Partnership
Project management by Deer Park Productions
Typeset by PDQ Typesetting
Printed and bound in Great Britain by Bell & Bain Ltd, Glasgow

Learning Matters Ltd
33 Southernhay East
Exeter EX1 1NX
Tel: 01392 215560
info@learningmatters.co.uk
www.learningmatters.co.uk

CONTENTS

ABWA	audit by walking around
ADSL	asymmetrical digital subscriber line
BBC	British Broadcasting Corporation
BECTa	British Educational Communications and Technology Agency
BETT	British Educational Training and Technology Show
CD-ROM	compact disc read-only memory
DfES	Department for Education and Skills
DVD	digital video disk or digital versatile disk
EC&T	Educational Computing & Technology
HTML	hyper-text markup language
ICT	information and communication/s technology
ILS	integrated learning system (usually)
ISDN	integrated services digital network
ISP	internet service provider
IT	information technology
LEA	local education authority
MAPE	(formerly) micros and primary education
NAACE	National Association of Advisers for Computers in Education
NGfL	National Grid for Learning
NLS	National Literacy Strategy
NOF	New Opportunities Fund
OFSTED	Office for Standards in Education
PDF	portable document format
PGCE	Postgraduate Certificate in Education
PIN	Parents' information network
QCA	Qualifications and Curriculum Authority
RAM	random access memory
RSI	repetitive strain injury
RTF	rich text format
SENCO	special educational needs co-ordinator
SMART	specific, measurable, achievable, realistic, timed
TRE	Teacher Resource Exchange
TTA	Teacher Training Agency
URL	uniform resource locator (previously 'universal')
VTC	virtual teacher centre
WLAN	wireless local area network
ZPD	zone of proximal development

It is assumed that you are reading this book because you wish to be (or perhaps already are) an ICT (information and communication technology) co-ordinator. What does an ICT co-ordinator need to do? What does he/she need to know? Why would a school need one? This book is written to give you some idea of what the role entails, and to offer you some suggestions about how you might go about it as effectively as possible.

Co-ordinating ICT in a primary school is not like co-ordinating other subjects, for a number of reasons. Though the work of other subject co-ordinators is generally considered to have a cross-curricular dimension (particularly in literacy), in no other subject does this dimension form the major part of what is to be done. In some respects it is like being a subject co-ordinator and special educational needs co-ordinator (SENCO) or assessment co-ordinator all rolled into one. Because of this one could argue that in terms of the staff hierarchy it should be considered a post of considerable seniority. In the past this has not often been the case unless the role has also been combined with that of, say, deputy head, though the rising status of ICT in the primary school may now be reflected in the improving status of the ICT co-ordinator, as we shall see in Chapter 2.

ICT makes demands upon its co-ordinator to adopt a wider variety of roles than any other subject. In particular it carries with it an expectation that one will exhibit technical know-how and act as an impromptu troubleshooter. You will be expected to keep abreast of innovations, and to mediate, filter and explain these to the senior management team and the rest of the staff. This goes beyond keeping up to date with the mountain of paperwork and new initiatives and directives that would be expected of the literacy or numeracy co-ordinator, since a substantial part of what you need to know to do the job really well does not come in pre-packaged form. You need to be adept at keeping your ear to the ground.

The Department for Education and Skills (DfES) currently uses the title 'subject leader' to describe the role that might otherwise be termed subject co-ordinator. Throughout this book the terms will be interchangeable. The role of subject leader is described in *The Teachers' Standards Framework* (DfES, 2001).[41] This is a one-size-fits-all description, and it is supposed to apply equally to, say, the head of a science department in a large secondary school and the teacher who is responsible for three or four subjects and the co-ordination of a whole key stage in a tiny village primary school. The *Framework* says:

> *Subject leaders provide professional leadership and management for a subject to secure high quality teaching, effective use of resources and improved standards of learning and achievement for all pupils.*

It then lists attributes, roles and expectations under ten headings, with a total of 44 bullet points, to which this book will make reference. You may consider some to be of no more than peripheral relevance to you in your role. However, it should become apparent that the role of the ICT co-ordinator also extends into areas not covered in those standards. It is worth noting at this point that the *Framework* itself is entirely voluntary, though its structure and assumptions are currently being adopted by many schools.

Just to complicate matters, there is a growing awareness that perhaps the roles of ICT subject leader and ICT co-ordinator are *not* the same. The advice from OFSTED (2002a)[68] is:

> *The co-ordination of ICT demands a considerable range of expertise, requiring good ICT understanding and knowledge, technical skills and the ability to provide professional support. Too many demands are placed on some ICT co-ordinators, most of whom have a full teaching commitment and few opportunities for monitoring the subject adequately across the school. In recognition of the demands of the role, larger primary, middle and secondary schools increasingly have more than one member of staff involved in the co-ordination of ICT.*

This is a clear recognition of the growing importance of ICT within education in general. The British Educational Communications and Technology Agency (BECTa)[6] suggests that schools need to consider having ICT co-ordination carried out by a senior school manager who oversees a range of ICT roles undertaken by specialists. For smaller primary schools, separating the roles is probably a luxury they will not be able to afford – except in the sense that a high proportion of ICT co-ordinators go on to be promoted to deputy headships and headships, so in the fullness of time we might expect it to become more common for the deputy head to have the background and experience to be able to take responsibility for the strategic management of ICT, and leave the day-to-day management of resources, schemes of work and so forth to a more junior colleague.

A book of this size cannot cover all there is to say about co-ordinating ICT in a twenty-first century primary school, and inevitably, as with everything else to do with ICT, parts of it will be overtaken by innovations fairly rapidly.

The following chapters address key skills and issues to do with being an ICT co-ordinator in a primary school. Each is structured in a similar way beginning with the specific National Standards for Subject Leaders (taken from the *Teachers' Standards Framework*) that will be addressed in that chapter. Questions are included throughout to help you reflect on your current situation and future professional development, and references to printed and electronic resources are included to help you develop in your role. Most of these references are to web addresses: these are listed in the Resources section at the end of the book, and for the sake of simplicity are identified in the body of the text by means of a number within square brackets.

1 A BRIEF BACKGROUND

Some things in education are very slow to change. Despite an apparently unceasing welter of new initiatives from the government and elsewhere in recent years, in many respects schools have changed very little. Imagine you were teaching a little over twenty years ago and had been given a time machine in which you projected yourself to the present day. What differences would you notice? Firstly, the doors of the school would be locked, and you would not be at liberty to wander in; next, you might find more adults around than you expected – particularly classroom assistants. Then you might notice a higher incidence of school uniforms and a lower incidence of open-plan classrooms. You might notice a lot more ring binders on shelves in the staff room. You might notice a difference in the way children's work was presented on the walls – certainly, you might be surprised by the relative absence of handwritten work. In most respects, though, things would be much as you would expect – classrooms, cloakrooms, books, boards, tables, trays, cupboards, a lot of different apparatus of one sort or another.

Then you open the door to what you think of as the music practice room and, amazingly, the room is full of screens and keyboards – a computer suite. Twenty years ago you would probably not have predicted this. No primary school in the land could possibly afford equipment like this, and what could it possibly be *for*, anyway? And when you look closer at the classrooms, you see that there are computers there as well. A few rooms have projection devices fixed to the ceiling, and even the whiteboards plug in. It would seem nearly as unlikely as your time machine.

We have now had twenty years to acclimatise ourselves to the reality of information and communication technology (ICT) in primary schools:

- from the first tentative BBC 'B's in 1982, taken up eagerly by a few enthusiasts but practically ignored for several years by many teachers;

- through a seemingly interminable sequence of newer, bigger, faster machines with improving graphics capabilities and bigger and better storage devices;

- through a pupil: computer ratio that has improved by fits and starts, school fetes and government grants, from perhaps 1:400 to the 2002 figure of 1:11;

- through a pedagogy that started as a means of addressing the almost impossible task of providing adequate access for all pupils, with software that was limited in range and sophistication, to an increasingly coherent and well articulated justification for ICT in terms of current learning theory;

- through staff development opportunities which for years were limited and uneven, to the massive New Opportunities Fund (NOF) expenditure on training all teaching staff, which produced mixed and generally rather unsatisfactory results;

● through expectations that were, originally, not much more than developing a little 'computer awareness' among primary children, to the present position, where at least 75 per cent of homes with children of school age have a computer, and even small children come to school confidently knowing how to do some quite sophisticated things (bear in mind that less than twenty years ago teachers were going to after-school training sessions on how to use a disk drive), and the National Curriculum makes the use of ICT statutory, and Office for Standards in Education (OFSTED) inspectors expect to see ICT being put to effective use on a regular basis in teaching and learning in all classes;

● through the gradual expansion of the horizons of ICT in education as the internet evolves.

In many ways, the route from that first machine to the current situation where you can reasonably expect that schools are networked and children have internet access has been very haphazard, with many false starts and sidetracks. If you were to stop your time machine every four or five years on your journey and ask teachers to define what they thought the school computers were for, you would probably get a different answer each time – and there is no reason to suppose the answers will not be different again four years from now, and again after that, and so on. In the first version of the National Curriculum, information technology (IT) was not even a subject in its own right but a mere appendage to design and technology. As its role and importance have continued to develop, so it has emerged as a separate foundation subject in 1995 and as a central part of the curriculum since 2000. It is sometimes spoken of as a core subject, though technically it is not.

There has also been a developing recognition that ICT is both a subject in its own right and also a means to enhance and transform teaching and learning across the whole curriculum. There is a substantial overlap between these two senses of the term ICT, but there are also distinctions to be made, which sometimes get smothered in rhetoric. That is one of the central themes of this book.

2 THE ROLE OF THE ICT CO-ORDINATOR

(→) According to the National Standards for Subject Leadership, you should:

- have knowledge and understanding of the characteristics of high quality teaching and the main strategies for improving and sustaining high standards of teaching, learning and achievement for all pupils;

- have knowledge and understanding of the relationship of the subject to the curriculum as a whole;

- analyse and interpret relevant national, local and school data, research and inspection evidence, to inform policies, practices, expectations, targets and teaching methods;

- prioritise and manage own time effectively, particularly in relation to balancing the demands made by teaching, subject management and involvement in school development;

- establish staff and resource needs and advise the head teacher and senior managers of likely priorities for expenditure, and allocate available resources with maximum efficiency to meet the objectives of the school and subject plans and achieve value for money;

- ensure the effective and efficient management and organisation of learning resources, including information and communication technology;

- maintain existing resources and explore opportunities to develop or incorporate new resources from a wide range of sources inside and outside the school;

- ensure that the head teacher, senior managers and governors are well informed about subject policies, plans and priorities, the success in meeting objectives and targets, and subject-related professional development plans.

Reflection

In principle, all 44 bullet points in the National Standards for Subject Leadership are intended to apply to the role of the ICT co-ordinator. If you have access to a copy of the Framework, read all the points. Can you identify any which do not really apply to you?

What does the role include?

As we have seen in the introduction, the position of the ICT co-ordinator and/or subject leader in the school hierarchy has become slightly ambiguous. Whereas in the past the role was often seen as relatively junior, the increasing importance of ICT in the curriculum, and the sheer size of the ICT budget, have made the role more demanding than it was.

According to BECTa,[6] the task cannot be entirely undertaken by one person, but parts of it will need to be delegated. The contention of this book is that as ICT becomes more embedded in the curriculum and in all teachers' perceptions of their role, this delegation will be easier to accomplish. Part of your task will be to move this process forward.

BECTa identifies the key roles of the ICT co-ordinator as:

- raising standards in ICT as a National Curriculum subject, by:
  - establishing a scheme of work;
  - training and supporting staff;
  - assembling and producing resources;
  - identifying effective ways of teaching using ICT;
- co-ordinating ICT across the whole curriculum;
- managing the school's ICT resources, including:
  - sorting out faults and problems with hardware and software;
  - installing and configuring software;
  - advising on new purchases and replacement of consumables;
  - management of the network;
  - overseeing the inventory of ICT resources;
  - internet filtering;
- reviewing the ICT policy;
- advising the head teacher on the development plan.

What do schools actually ask for?

A survey of 15 job specifications for primary ICT co-ordinator vacancies early in 2003 revealed the following information.

- The schools (nine primary, four junior, two infant) had an average of 348 children on roll, with a range of 210–560. This is not representative of the country as a whole, as there were no small schools present. In very small schools the role of ICT co-ordinator is much more likely to be combined with other duties and perhaps the co-ordination of more subjects. One school had Beacon status, and one was in special measures. About half of the schools were in or near London.

- Two schools offered three management points to suitable candidates, six offered two points, four offered one and three did not specify what was on offer. One school stated that the vacancy was a senior management post, and three others implied it; two schools described the post as middle management.

- Two schools asked for a minimum of five years' teaching experience, three asked for three years and one asked for two years. The other nine did not specify, but none suggested the post was suitable for a newly qualified teacher.

- Ten schools stated explicitly that the appointee would be expected to be an excellent classroom practitioner who could lead by example.

- All the job descriptions mentioned managing ICT across the whole school, and supporting and advising other colleagues. Thirteen schools referred to managing in-service training.

- Eleven schools made reference to monitoring planning, teaching and/or assessment, and nine mentioned the maintenance of a school ICT portfolio.

- Thirteen schools mentioned the maintenance of hardware and other resources and most related this to the management of a budget.

- The expectation that the appointee would keep abreast of developments in ICT was explicitly stated by eight schools.

- Maintenance or writing of the school ICT policy was mentioned by nine schools; five also referred to the writing or presenting of reports, e.g. to the governors.

- Informing parents about ICT was mentioned by seven schools, though none referred to making resources or training available.

- No school referred specifically to liaison with classroom assistants to support the maintenance and implementation of ICT.

- Four schools made some reference to extra-curricular ICT activities for children.

- Support for student teachers was mentioned by two schools; nobody mentioned support for newly qualified teachers.

- Four schools made reference to the maintenance of displays involving ICT, but only two schools referred to the running of the school website and only two to the maintenance of the network.

- Only two schools made mention of the provision of release time from teaching in order to fulfil the responsibilities of the post. A 1999 DfES statistical survey found that 18 per cent of primary ICT co-ordinators had non-contact time averaging two hours.[36]

Blending teaching and technology

Perhaps you have had a burning desire for many years to be a primary school ICT co-ordinator. Many people enter primary teaching because, consciously or not, they want to emulate a teacher they greatly admired when they were themselves a primary pupil, and we have perhaps had computers in primary schools for long enough now that one might remember an inspirational and innovative ICT-using teacher from one's own formative years.

Alternatively, some ICT co-ordinators never consciously expected to take on the role at all. The thought had never entered their head until they arrived late for a staff meeting one day and found they had been enthusiastically nominated for the post by their colleagues, not necessarily because they showed any specific aptitude for the subject. Several years ago there were certainly genuine instances where this had happened. At least one ICT co-ordinator was appointed on the basis of being the only member of staff to have colour printouts on the classroom wall. In some cases the teacher who got lumbered went on to be a first-rate ICT co-ordinator – perhaps partly because they did not intimidate their colleagues with technical jargon, and did not adopt the mantle of the One Who Knows, so they immediately created a sense of joint ownership.

More likely, you have been an enthusiastic user of ICT for a while, and have also had a desire to be a primary teacher for a while, and the two strands have coalesced into your present course of action.

A large proportion of students entering initial teacher training (ITT) now feel themselves to be generally confident and competent users of ICT for their own purposes, and most own, or have access to, a relatively up-to-date computer. Almost without exception, students are familiar with at least the basic functions of a word processor. Whereas five years ago most new teaching students had little or no experience of the internet and e-mail, new students for whom that is true are now very rare (Fox, 2002).[47]

It should go without saying that an ICT co-ordinator should like working with computers and other technology. You will not be happy in the job if this is not true. It does not necessarily follow that you need to have a lot of technical knowledge – nobody is going to expect you to build your own computers from scratch, or disassemble Microsoft Office – but everyone will expect that you have some technical understanding, and probably that you know something that they do not. You would expect an airline pilot to have a fundamental grasp of aerodynamics and some generally reliable ideas about the geography of the world, but you would not expect them to be able to design a jet engine or describe in detail the main industries of Burkina Faso.

However, it is more important that you have a good grasp of how classrooms and schools are organised and what effective teaching and learning look like. In fact, it is of paramount importance that you are a good teacher first and foremost. If your passion for technology outweighs your desire to educate and enthuse young minds, you are probably in the wrong job. If your enthusiasm for the technology becomes detached from the core business of teaching and learning, you will not be an effective ICT co-ordinator. The computer is in school to serve the needs of the curriculum, not to be its master. That is not to say, however, that you should restrict the curriculum to what could be done without a computer. An important part of your role is to demonstrate how ICT can transform teaching and learning, and to think imaginatively about how new and emerging technologies might play a useful role in curriculum development.

You will serve your school and your colleagues best if you can establish your credentials as a good teacher with or without the aid of technology, but also visibly set an example in the use of technology in your own practice. This does not mean that you should always have first access to the newest equipment, or that you should permit your colleagues to expect that this will be the case. Particularly, do not hoard ICT equipment – this has been a weakness of ICT co-ordinators in the past. What schools do not need is a techie whizzkid who dazzles everybody else with know-how and talks in impenetrable jargon. In short, don't be a geek.

Being the One Who Knows

It's nice being the One Who Knows. People bring their queries to you, assuming you are more likely to be able to give a definitive answer than anyone else in the immediate vicinity. People trust your judgement. Your opinion seems to count for quite a lot, whether or not you really know anything. It's all very flattering, very good for the ego.

A lot of schools have treated their ICT co-ordinator in these terms, because there is a certain amount of truth in the surmise. You *do* know things that others don't, about the way the technology works and about the place of ICT in the development of learning and teaching, and you have reached some understandings that for the moment at least seem to elude others. Added to that, ICT is a very *cool* subject in the eyes of most children, and you have been identified as its foremost exponent in the school, which should give you a certain amount of kudos.

However, one of your main tasks, which is never actually spelt out in the job description, is to rise above all this, to seek to ensure that others, collectively, know what you know, and thus perhaps ultimately to render significant parts of your role unnecessary.

Creating and leaving a shadow

If you are good at what you do, you will be an influence for good throughout the school in terms of the way in which ICT is deployed and used. You will lead by example, and it is hoped that some of the good examples you set will be reflected in changes in the practices of colleagues, and that these changes will come to form part of the natural repertoire of those colleagues, so that they will continue to work in those ways long after you have moved on to your deputy headship or whatever you are destined to do next. However, there is evidence that this does not always happen, and when innovative practitioners move on, they do not 'leave a shadow'. This is particularly true if what the innovative practitioner does is very different from what others do. Perhaps this is very arrogant and based on massive assumptions about one's worth – but it is a good idea to plan to ensure that you have a shadow.

How might you do this?

- Try not to keep information to yourself about where things are kept or how they work. Make sure that at least one colleague knows the answers to mundane issues like where the blank disks are kept.

- You should not write down your most secret passwords, but do make sure that someone else has access to everything you have access to. Do not be the only person to have administrator rights to the network. You can be quite sure that the day you are away on a course, or in a hospital delivery room, is the day that the network will grind to a halt.

- Cultivate your friends. Make sure you have made yourself sufficiently well understood to at least one other colleague so that when you depart you will leave a shadow.

Reflection

Can you identify anything about what you know about computers or ICT that you are fairly certain nobody else in your school knows? Make a list.
How might you share this knowledge?

Liaising with others

Do not lose sight of the fact that there are thousands of other primary ICT co-ordinators in the country. Many are working in schools that are very much like yours, with children and teachers very much like yours, with the same curriculum objectives as you, and using the same software and very similar hardware to yours. Many know a lot of things about ICT that you do not know (yet, at least). Probably, most are more experienced than you. It is clearly to your advantage to have some insight into their thinking and their mode of operation. Many have been faced with the same problems as you, and in some cases have solved them in ways you could benefit from knowing about.

- Find out about local user groups. If your school is part of a cluster or pyramid, are there existing structures for staff liaison? There is some advantage in having knowledgeable and like-minded colleagues within easy reach. If no such structure exists, when the opportunity arises, offer to help in setting one up. At the very least, exchange e-mail addresses with your neighbours.

- If you work in a school that receives children from an earlier stage (e.g. if yours is a junior school), find out about how ICT is provided for in the feeder school or schools. It is important that you have a good grasp of what children's prior experience of ICT in school has been, what software and hardware they are already familiar with, what skills they have and what standards they have reached.

- Get to know how ICT is managed and delivered in the schools your pupils go on to. Respect what they do, but do not be overwhelmed by the differences in the way you operate – their priorities are not the same as yours – and particularly, do not allow yourself to be pressured into changing what seems to you to be good primary practice in order to fit in with their agenda. There are for example situations where primary schools' networks are administered from the local secondary school. Though some advantages may be claimed for this in terms of economy and efficiency, it does represent a significant loss of autonomy by the primary school, and can in fact prove inefficient if, for example, you have to wait for the secondary school network manager to install new software you wish to use. If your school's relationship with the secondary school/s is well developed, there may already be arrangements in place for pupils to undertake transition projects, which they start in one school and finish in the other. ICT is an exceptionally useful tool in this context, and there clearly needs to be understanding, collaboration and discussion between ICT co-ordinators. Try to get involved in this work. If such an arrangement does not exist, sound out your colleagues to see if it could be a future possibility.

- Your local education authority (LEA) probably has an ICT advisory service. At the earliest opportunity you should seek to make personal contact with whoever has responsibility for supporting your school. It is very likely that there will be evening courses on aspects of primary ICT. If these are of a fairly technical nature, or are specifically targeted at ICT co-ordinators, then you should endeavour to attend in person. If they are more general, or, for example, about the use of ICT in a specific curriculum subject, then encourage your colleagues to attend, and feed back information to you afterwards (or better still, disseminate it to everyone at a staff meeting). Some LEAs run training days specifically for ICT co-ordinators, and you should make attendance at these a high priority. Apart from the obvious fact that you should thereby develop your own ICT skills and understanding, there is much to be gained from networking with others – all teachers know that coffee and lunch are often very useful parts of such days. If there is no e-mail group for primary ICT co-ordinators, get together with others and set one up. Be willing to exchange teaching ideas, technical hints and tips, perhaps resources you have developed. Do not use it for illegal purposes like exchange of copyright software. It is absolutely essential that the good example you set to others includes being scrupulous about this – piracy is theft, and the consequences for your school and for your future career are dire. Increasingly, with software that has an online dimension, it is traceable.

- Your LEA may run, or contribute to, a site associated with the National Grid for Learning (NGfL). If you are in Farmshire, this is likely to be called the Farmshire Grid for Learning, and abbreviated to FGfL. At present these sites vary considerably in size, scope and purpose, but most have links to websites or downloadable resources, often of local interest; many are portals to in-service course details and bookings; some have ongoing projects to which you or your children can contribute. Get to know your local site, and find out what you could gain from it and what you can contribute.

- Involve yourself with other agencies and organisations – see Chapter 3. The Virtual Teacher Centre, which is technically part of the NGfL, has a conferencing area, which should have been a major contribution to ongoing discussions about the role of ICT, but in the few years of its life so far it has not really caught fire in the way it was intended to – some discussion threads barely get started, some have very infrequent additions, and some have tended to be dominated by a small handful of individuals. What seems to work rather better are the occasional online conferences, which characteristically run for about two days and which engage the services of a number of experts to make presentations and to remain online for most of the conference to respond to messages from other 'delegates'. The presentations and ensuing discussions remain online afterwards. For example, see the documents provided by BECTa.[11]

Reflection

Take each of the above points in turn. What connections do you already have? Can you design a medium-term action plan to extend your range of contacts? If you already know some other ICT co-ordinators, what do they know (or have) that would be useful to you? What do you know (or have) that would be useful to them?

Managing a budget

By comparison with other subjects, a school's overall annual expenditure on ICT is normally very large. This is because:

● the primary school pupil:computer ratio is continuing to improve, which of course means that the number of computers in a school is continuing to rise, with an expected ratio of 8:1 by 2004;

● computer hardware is still expensive, and needs maintaining and replacing on a regular basis (see Chapter 7);

● there is a growing expectation that classrooms will be equipped with expensive items like data projectors and interactive whiteboards;

● though there are many good resources available free of charge on the internet, the cost of educational software has risen considerably in real terms, particularly with a gradual move from site licences to multi-user licences.

The first computers in primary schools were half-funded by the Department of Trade and Industry (DTI). Then, for a few years, a lot of money from school fetes and bazaars went towards increasing the stock. Major expansions in school equipment came about largely as a result of government grants, either through LEAs or directly to schools – see Chapter 4 for information about the DfES Standards Fund. As time has gone on, there has been a gradual acceptance that the cost of good ICT pro-vision in schools is high, but unavoidable. Government investment in ICT in schools is currently huge, and it is difficult to see how it could ever be substantially reduced now.

You must expect that, even in a school that values ICT highly, there may be pockets of resentment among your colleagues at that level of expenditure. This is understand-able; you can buy a lot of books for the cost of an interactive whiteboard. However, try not to take it personally – if it seems to be aimed at you, then perhaps you are too closely identified with ICT, as the One Who Knows about ICT.

Decisions about capital expenditure on new computers, printers, etc. will probably be made by the head teacher or deputy head, in consultation with you, and in accordance with the medium- or long-term plan expressed in the school ICT policy and/ or the ICT development plan (see Chapter 4). You may well have more immediate control over the budget for software and consumables. At the very least, you will be expected to make recommendations about what to buy, which of course should also be consonant with the medium-term plan in the ICT policy in general terms, though you would be wise to ensure that you have discussed with colleagues what they think would meet their current needs. It is always as well to retain a small contingency fund if you can to meet any unforeseen expenditure.

You should know what happens to machines that are sent for repair and how this is paid for. This should be a separate fund from the software budget, so that planned development of curriculum software cannot be scuppered because someone's monitor goes on the blink.

It may well be that you are operating within a managed service (see Chapter 7), in which case the overall figure for expenditure on hardware, maintenance and repair will have been agreed beforehand.

Confidence and bluff

Nobody knows everything there is to know about the technical aspects of ICT in education; as time goes on and things become ever more sophisticated, the percentage that even the best informed know about is dwindling.

One of the assumptions your colleagues will make about you, which is entirely unreasonable, is that you will automatically know everything there is to know about a new piece of software (or new hardware) the moment it arrives, or that your favourite way of relaxing in the evening is with a stack of software manuals so that you can support them. This assumption is more likely to be made if you always appear supremely confident. Confidence is more likely to be based on a strong sense that, in general terms, most modern software is very intuitive and easy to navigate, so you should be able to work out what to do on the spot, or, if you can't, you should be able to try things out speculatively, with a reasonable chance of success. When adults say that children are naturally good with computers, this is normally what they mean − that children are prepared to try things out and click on things to see what happens.

Confidence is also about:

- familiarity with conventions, so that, say, in Windows programs, you know there will be a menu bar at the top of the screen, and 'Open', 'Save', 'Print' options will all be found if you click on 'File';
- recognising icons for common activities − so clicking on an icon of a floppy disk will save your file.

Mostly, you do not need to teach this sort of thing to children in a systematic manner

– familiarity develops naturally with usage. However, as we shall see, when assessing children's ICT capabilities, it is easy to be fooled by the apparent level of confidence into an assumption of general competence when in fact there may be some misconceptions to overcome.

There is a well-known saying in educational computing circles: 'If all else fails, consult the manual'. Having a go is all very well, and will get you started in most contexts, but, particularly with software tools as opposed to games or instructional programs, there is always the possibility that there are valuable functions you simply don't discover for yourself.

Teachers often say something to the effect of, 'ICT is fine when it's all running smoothly, but as soon as anything goes wrong, I'm just lost.' This is the point at which they assume that you will be able to fix things for them, as if by magic, even though you have never seen this particular piece of software before or the printer is making inexplicable funny noises. If you value your reputation as the One Who Knows, and if you have time to get involved, you will resort to a mixture of bluff and common sense.

Reflection

Make a list of things you know you don't know about the use of ICT in the primary school that you think you should know. What can you do about this?

What would be your priorities, and what things are you prepared to go on not knowing?

Managing your time

At the time of writing, there are plans afoot to provide all primary teachers with some non-contact time. This is vastly overdue, and may have a significant impact on your capacity to fulfil your role effectively.

In the past, ICT co-ordinators have generally had charge of their own classes every morning and every afternoon, with perhaps a little leeway for, say, hymn practice. The more fortunate have been granted a small amount of breathing space while someone else takes their class for music or swimming or whatever. Small gaps such as these are all too often swallowed up in day-to-day classroom management issues, and you have to be quite strict with yourself and all your colleagues if you want to dedicate them consistently to something else.

There will be an expectation that you will be prepared to work before school, after school, during breaktimes and lunchtimes, to keep the system ticking over. If your school has breakfast clubs, lunchtime computer access and after-school computer clubs, you will no doubt be expected to run those, or at least be on hand to act as a troubleshooter. If you can accommodate these activities in your schedule, then by all means take them on, but they are actually a good way to bring on the confidence and competence of inexperienced colleagues. It is quite good policy to ask someone else to look after them, and simply maintain a watching brief or drop in occasionally to see how things are going.

Your colleagues will want you to sort out little problems for them. This tends to happen at the start of lessons, when something being set up does not do what it was expected to do. This can be very frustrating for you, as you have your own lesson to start. In an ideal world all schools would have a dedicated full-time ICT technician, whose job it would be to sort out these matters. In practice, though there is an increasing likelihood that you will have a part share in a technician (perhaps for one day per week), it is unlikely that the ideal position will be reached in the near future. In order to maintain the fragile levels of confidence you have been nurturing in colleagues, you may well consider it a sound investment to take staples out of printers, hunt out a backup disk or push the monitor connection cable back into its socket.

Reflection

What are you really confident about?

Many apparent computer problems have simple, common-sense solutions. If a colleague tells you the printer will not print, what checks would you carry out and in what order?

Reflection

How do you see the role of the ICT co-ordinator in the primary school? What are your priorities? Look at the NAACE Tool to determine the priorities of the ICT co-ordinator's role[59]. You might wish to read the rest of this book before coming to any conclusions.

Summary

To be an effective ICT co-ordinator, you need to:

- take responsibility for standards in ICT throughout the school;
- oversee the ICT scheme of work;
- co-ordinate ICT across the whole curriculum;
- support and train colleagues in their use of ICT;
- manage ICT resources;
- establish and evaluate the school ICT policy.

As a priority, you should seek to ensure that ICT is embedded in the general practice of the school.

(→) According to the National Standards for Subject Leadership, you should:

- have knowledge and understanding of the relationship of the subject to the curriculum as a whole;
- prioritise and manage own time effectively, particularly in relation to balancing the demands made by teaching, subject management and involvement in school development;
- achieve challenging professional goals;
- take responsibility for your own professional development;
- ensure that there is a safe working and learning environment in which risks are properly assessed.

Rapid development

An obvious point about ICT is that it is in a state of constant and rapid development:

- Firstly in terms of the speed and capacity of computers. Moore's Law states that the number of transistors on a microprocessor will double approximately every 18 months. This conventionally translates into the assertion that computers will double in capacity and speed over the same time period, and for many years this rule seems to have been remarkably accurate. Similarly, much faster internet access via broadband makes the rapid transfer of large amounts of information possible.
- Secondly in terms of the development and progressive affordability of other devices. Twenty years ago a simple floppy disk drive cost over £100; today a much better drive might cost £10–15. Ten years ago, a reasonable scanner could cost over £1,000; today computer sellers throw in a scanner as a 'free gift'. Computers are sold in price brackets: the actual price of computer does not vary much, but month after month the specification gets better and the numbers (for processor speed, memory, disk capacity, speed of CD-ROM drive, etc.) get larger.
- Thirdly in terms of innovations in resources. For example, the internet has developed from being a text-only medium, through a phase where it was dominated by graphics, to a phase where, via the medium of plug-ins like Flash, ShockWave or QuickTime, sound, video and complex interactive animations are becoming conventional.

- Fourthly in terms of expectations, particularly from the DfES.

- Fifthly in terms of the massive increase in home ownership of computers in recent years, which means that many children spend far more time on ICT-related activities at home than they do at school.[15] See Chapter 9.

Keeping up to date

As ICT co-ordinator, you will need to keep abreast of these developments, to report on them to the senior management team and other colleagues, and also because you owe it to your pupils to be well informed. Some of the children will have better computers at home than you have in school, and some will have parents who are apparently very well informed about new innovations and who will no doubt wish to tell you about them. Every few months there seems to be an eruption of new TLAs (three-letter acronyms) that computer people bandy about as though they had always been in existence ('... so I saved it as RTF, HTML and PDF, and uploaded the URL to my ISP... '). As you absorb these, keep your own glossary of terms, and make it available in the staffroom, with simple down-to-earth descriptions or explanations if possible. If you decide to develop an ICT handbook (see Chapter 4), it should be included there.

Keep up to date by liaising and networking with others, as described in Chapter 2. Subscribe to an educational computing magazine like InterActive. If possible, leave this lying around on the staffroom table. The Times Educational Supplement has a regular OnLine supplement every two months with which you should be familiar. See the Resources section at the end of this book for useful links and other sources of ideas.

Finding and disseminating resources on the web

The importance of the internet to education, and specifically to your role, is increasing daily. Though it contains an enormous amount of material that is of no relevance at all to you, and, distressingly, a large amount that is downright offensive, it is becoming impossible to ignore it as a major source of information and resources. You will be expected to have extensive knowledge of it. You will not be able to keep abreast of everything – however efficient you are, this would be a full-time occupation in itself.

Be familiar with more than one search engine. Google[49] is probably your best starting place currently, but other search engines work in different ways and might be useful; look, for example, at Kartoo.[52] Develop your skills at searching efficiently, and pass these skills on to colleagues and children.

Keep a list of websites that are worth keeping an eye on. You might decide simply to store these in your Favourites or Bookmarks, but it is also a good idea to have an annotated list, to remind you why the sites are worth visiting. If you have Microsoft Word or a similar word processor, open a new file whenever you conduct an online trawl of the most productive websites, and copy and paste anything that might be of interest to you or any of your colleagues later. Remember to copy and paste the address, particularly if it is a link to an online activity. Add whatever annotation you need to remind you why you wanted to save it, and save the file with a meaningful filename that also includes the date of the trawl. This approach will support you if you find yourself following up interesting links that go off at tangents from what you were looking for. Be prepared to surf a little – many productive avenues of enquiry come about serendipitously.

Get into the habit of e-mailing useful links to colleagues. Much time gets wasted by people miscopying or mistyping URLs and not arriving where they intended, so it is quicker to give people something to click on, and to improve everyone's skills in copying and pasting or at least using *Favourites* or *Bookmarks*, so that they can maintain their own lists. It is also good policy to give out the message that good ICT practice can speed up processes and reduce errors. Your task is to know about the major resources and to pass useful information to your colleagues – but don't simply do their work for them. Your ear should be to the ground to a greater extent than theirs, but you are not their support assistant.

It is also sometimes possible to motivate colleagues to make greater or more efficient use of the internet by setting an example. When a colleague asks you if you know any good ICT resources to support, say, the work on frogs, a well-executed search that finds something useful more or less straightaway can be a powerful motivator. As the internet continues to expand rapidly, there will increasingly be excellent resources and teaching materials, freely available, that you have not seen before. Be slightly wary of non-UK sources. In particular, with websites from the USA, be sensitive to American spellings and vocabulary, cultural assumptions, references to flora and fauna, and so forth (… *Last Thanksgiving I saw a raccoon on the sidewalk* …).

There is a wide range of websites containing resources for primary teachers, including large quantities of off-the-peg lesson plans and ideas, worksheets, PowerPoint presentations and web-based materials. You will no doubt already be familiar with several. A useful source of such materials is the Teacher Resource Exchange (TRE), which is part of the Virtual Teacher Centre (VTC).[89] Note in particular the free games and resources available from:

- the BBC site;[3]
- GridClub[50] (see also Chapter 9);
- the Infant Explorer site;[51]
- the MAPE site.[54]

Reflection

Desert Island Websites: if you woke up tomorrow and found that almost all of the internet had vanished and you were left with just eight educational websites, which eight would you prefer them to be?

Compare notes with another ICT co-ordinator.

MAPE

If your school is not a member of MAPE, you should consider joining. MAPE originally stood for Micros And Primary Education, though now it does not officially stand for anything, as the term 'micros' is considered extremely dated. It is the largest primary school user group for ICT, with a membership of around 2,000, most of which are school memberships. In the past, MAPE had strong regional groups, who laid on events for members to find out about new hardware and software, but this has largely ceased now (except in Scotland, where it still thrives). MAPE membership entitles you to at least three publications per year, some of which are focused on the use of ICT in specific curriculum areas. Many contributions to MAPE publications are from practising teachers writing about innovative work they have done in their schools. There is an annual MAPE conference, just before Easter.

Curriculum Online

You should also know about Curriculum Online.[32] The website is a portal to a large online catalogue of software and resources to support learning and teaching across the curriculum, referenced against the National Curriculum and the Qualifications and Curriculum Authority (QCA) schemes of work. The DfES provides funding for schools in the form of *eLearning Credits*, which can be used to purchase extra software and resources via the Curriculum Online site. The money is ringfenced, and cannot be used for any other purpose. The probability is that you will have a major say in how that money is spent, and you should spend some time browsing the Curriculum Online site to get a feel for what might be available, so that you will be able to offer your colleagues effective support and ensure that the software requirements of the whole curriculum are being met and are being kept in reasonable balance.

BETT and the Education Show

Persuade your head teacher that, in terms of your professional development, providing a day's supply cover so that you can visit the British Educational Training and Technology (BETT) exhibition in January and/or the Education Show in March is money well spent. BETT is devoted entirely to educational ICT, and is the largest such exhibition in Europe. The Education Show has a much broader remit, but there is a substantial amount of ICT content. Both have a seminar programme in which leading experts and representatives of major organisations and agencies like BECTa provide details of new initiatives or results of recent research. Government ministers make keynote speeches at these shows, in which they unveil new plans for future spending on ICT and so forth. There are hundreds of stands at these exhibitions, which range from major players like government agencies and large firms like Microsoft or Apple, through medium-sized educational software specialists like Logotron or Sherston Software, to small organisations and kitchen-table firms. Large stands tend to have a schedule of demonstrations of their major products, and the specialist software firms have friendly assistants whose function is to give you a first-hand view of what their current products do and to answer your queries about them. It is impossible to come away from the BETT exhibition without a head full of stimulating ideas, probably an extended wish-list of future purchases, and a large carrier bag full of brochures, demonstration CD-ROMs, mouse mats and free pens.

Persuade your head teacher to let you go. Better still, persuade your head teacher to come with you.

Though on a much smaller scale than BETT or the Education Show, the Educational Computing & Technology (EC&T) Resource Conference in Doncaster in November is also worth a visit. There are also other regional conferences for which you will no doubt receive flyers.

Catalogues from leading software suppliers will arrive at your school regularly. There may be a designated place for storing these. It is sometimes a good idea to leave a few lying around in the staffroom.

You will receive lots of unsolicited mail from firms trying to sell you their ICT-related goods and services. Most of it will be of no direct relevance to you, particularly if you have good links with your LEA and visit the BETT exhibition. You will need to make snap decisions about what to throw away immediately and what to keep in case it comes in handy. It is a good idea to keep a file for the latter group, and empty it every year or perhaps every six months.

The important point to note from the above is that you do not have to know everything about everything. Quite a lot of what people from outside the world of education talk about when they discuss ICT (they never call it that) is of no more than marginal relevance to you. Remember that you are probably the school enthusiast – and nobody else is keeping up in the same way that you are, and part of your job is to mediate it all to them.

The super-technician

You are not a super-technician. Your role is to be a teacher, and to help your colleagues to make effective use of ICT in their classrooms. Though you should of course have a basic familiarity with what plugs in where, opening the case of a computer or printer to add, alter or repair something does not fall within your remit, and it should be clearly understood by all colleagues and stakeholders that this is the case. If you do have knowledge and expertise in this area, by all means make use of it, but do so discreetly. If colleagues come to perceive you as a repairman, you can find a disproportionate amount of your time taken up in being just that, to the detriment of your class teaching; breaktimes will become a thing of the past.

On the other hand, much can be achieved by the rigid application of common sense. It is sometimes surprising how intelligent, educated adults can miss the simplest of things. This is a true story:

Teacher: 'I've set up this printer and it doesn't work.'

Me: 'Right, let's have a look. Where's the mains lead?'
Teacher: 'Mains lead?'

If you switch the printer on and no lights come on, swap the mains lead with another printer, and see which one comes on. If *this* lead works on *that* printer, then the fault is not in the lead. If it does not, but *that* lead works in *this* printer, then it is a fault in the lead. Check the fuse in the plug – and so on.

These situations will arise. Make a snap judgement – can I solve this problem quickly and simply? What difference will it make to my colleague's confidence and belief in the usefulness of ICT if I solve it now? Unless it is quick and simple and will have a positive effect, be prepared to be hard-hearted – it will pay dividends in the long run.

Health and safety

Your employer has the legal responsibility for ensuring that health and safety requirements are met. It is essential that you are familiar with basic health and safety issues related to the use of ICT. This is such a fundamental consideration that they are enumerated here, and many will be referred to again later in the book. Make yourself familiar with them; it is useful for you to have them at your fingertips. Most will come as no surprise to you, and are common sense and similar to requirements in other areas. Wherever possible, do not accept working conditions that violate any of these rules, and do not be afraid to bring any issues that arise to the attention of your head teacher.

When the OFSTED inspectors come to call, they will be interested in the following areas of concern:

- electrical safety;
- excessive heat;
- reflection and glare from lights and windows;
- distracting background noise;
- inappropriate software without adequate training;
- inadequate space to lay out work or work in pairs;
- equipment arranged for user comfort.

They will wish to interview whoever is responsible for maintenance and safety. They will review repair and maintenance records. They will ask about the school's policy for acceptable use of e-mail and the internet (see Chapter 7). They will also want to know when and how pupils are taught about safe ICT use.

Electrical safety

Maintenance and testing of all electrical equipment is required by the Electricity at Work Regulations 1989. It is *not* your job to test or repair things – leave that to a qualified electrician – but obviously you should report anything like frayed cables or damaged plugs immediately. Fuses should have the correct rating. To an extent, the positioning of equipment will be conditioned by the proximity of power points, network points or telephone points. Do not leave wires trailing across a thoroughfare. If you must run cables, ensure that they are secure and covered. Do not overload power points, and avoid coiled cables which can generate heat. There should be a carbon dioxide fire extinguisher within easy reach of any ICT equipment.

Excessive heat

ICT equipment gives off heat, which can build up as the day progresses, particularly in an enclosed computer room. The room should be well ventilated or air conditioned, and the temperature should be kept between 18 and 24 degrees Celsius.

Reflection and glare from lights and windows

Monitors should be positioned to minimise reflections and glare from lights and windows. This probably means placing monitors at right angles to the window or with the window behind it. Failing that, you may need to use blinds or curtains to ensure that users do not have to look into glare. Monitors should be able to tilt and swivel. If you are fortunate enough to have a data projector, you should try to avoid looking directly at the light. This is easier to do if it is ceiling-mounted.

Distracting background noise

Background noise (mostly from fans) is almost unavoidable, particularly in an ICT room. Though it is desirable to have children working collaboratively, and therefore talking to each other, they may have to do so against a background of noisy software. Consider the potential advantages of using headphones if children are working independently, but bear in mind that these will inhibit collaborative work.

Inappropriate software without adequate training

It is difficult to know what health and safety hazard OFSTED have in mind here in a primary context. Cracked CD-ROMs or DVDs can shatter in high-speed drives; other peripheral equipment can be hazardous unless training and dire warnings are given – for instance, children should not place datalogging temperature probes in their mouths.

Inadequate space to lay out work or work in pairs

There should be enough room for more than one child at a time to work at a computer, with space for books, etc., with gangways and emergency exits left clear and no baggage left in the way.

Equipment arranged for user comfort

- Users should be able to adjust their position – the height of chairs should be adjustable, and should permit the user to sit with knees under the desk and thighs horizontal.

- The top of the monitor should be roughly at eye level, and users should be able to adjust screen brightness and contrast.

- Keyboards should have the option of being flat or tilted, and pupils should be taught to type with more than two fingers to avoid the risk of repetitive strain injury (RSI).

- Users should be able to take frequent short breaks away from the screen.

Further information can be found in the BECTa materials from which this section is derived;[14] for a fuller discussion, see John Woollard's material at the Southampton University PGCE site.[92]

Reflection

Either physically or else in your mind's eye, walk around the ICT facilities with which you are most familiar. How sure are you that all health and safety regulations and recommendations are being adhered to?

If they are not, what can you do to improve the situation?

The school website

There is now an expectation that every school will have a website. What is a primary school website actually for?

- It will undoubtedly be viewed as an online prospectus, and as such it needs to be smart, attractive, up to date and accurate. It will be viewed by prospective parents, applicants for teaching vacancies, student teachers, school governors and parents, and probably OFSTED inspectors. At the DfES Parents' Centre website[34] you can type in your postcode and receive a list of all schools in your vicinity, with links to their School Performance Tables data, their OFSTED reports and their school websites. The message is clear to any head teacher or school governor: use your website to sell yourself.

- On the other hand, you will probably want the school website to be a working document for children to use, as a location for them to present their work and achievements, and perhaps as a resource base.

Good school websites manage to reconcile these conflicting interests, mainly through careful site design, so that users' attention is drawn to the things they are particularly looking for.

Of course, it is not necessarily your job to maintain the school website, and as we saw in the previous chapter, this function does not seem to rate highly in schools' job descriptions at present, but it might fall to you because:

- you enjoy creating web pages;
- no one else feels sufficiently confident to do it.

You would be well advised not to attempt to keep it to yourself.

BECTa[19] recommends that a senior member of staff has overall responsibility for the site, *checking legal issues, obtaining parents' permission to publish work, and ensuring that it presents your school as you wish it to be seen.* It also recommends that you set up an editorial team on a monthly rota, involving staff and children in the development of the site. Having a team has some advantages, as you get more than one pair of eyes on overall layout, and no single person should need to burn the midnight oil to keep it running.

On a regular basis the editor should read through the entire site, check that links work, and remove any material that is out of date. Many school websites get started in a wave of enthusiasm, and then neglected. There is no bigger turn-off than reading, *We hope you like our exciting new website, and we have big plans for 1999 ...*

Some schools pass control of their website to a parent or governor who perhaps has some professional involvement in web page creation or who maintains a website as a hobby. This has some obvious advantages, but editorial control should be retained within the school, and you should remember that commercial and hobbyist websites are both developed for purposes which are not identical to yours, and their design rationale is based on different principles.

If your school does not already have an adequate website, it is worth your while spending some time over its design and specification. Involve all the stakeholders in this process. That includes the head teacher and senior management team, teaching colleagues and classroom assistants, governors, parents and children. If you get the structure right, you will save a lot of time in the longer term. Also, if you give everyone a sense of ownership, the site will be easier to run, and more people will contribute to it.

Do not get saddled with it as a chore. If you do end up doing most of the work on it, remember that many effective sites are in fact very simple and do not need to be riddled with gimmicks. If you are an enthusiast for Flash, by all means make use of it; if you want to incorporate Javascript, you can obtain complete routines from the web and build them into your site, even if your understanding of HTML is only minimal. If you are substantially responsible for running the website, it is probably a good idea to have at least a nodding acquaintance with how HTML works – it really is not all that difficult.

It is absolutely imperative that you have a clearly understood policy about privacy and safety with regard to putting pictures of children onto your website.

- You must not put any pictures of children onto your site without express permission from parents.
- Most people would accept that you can include pictures of whole classes or large groups, including, for example, scenes from your school play.

- Shots taken from behind children's heads are normally acceptable. A common example is a picture of two children sitting at a computer.

- Do not include any personal details about children on your website. This probably includes not putting their names beside group pictures.

Responsibility for policy in this area rests with the governors and the head teacher. You should be sensitive and circumspect, but removing children's pictures altogether may feel like an admission of defeat.[38] [40]

From the outset, you should aim to make your site as accessible as possible to all users. This includes adding meta-tags to all illustrations so that visually impaired users, who might use special software to read the page aloud, can know what the pictures are. Industry-standard web page creation software like Dreamweaver now has the facility to check your page automatically, and remind you when you need to modify something or provide extra information.

BECTa and *The Guardian* run the annual National School and College Website Awards.[29] It would be worthwhile to have a look at the websites of prizewinners in the primary categories, to get some ideas about what your school website could perhaps be like.

Reflection

What do you think are the most important features of a good school website?

Look at the websites of a few other schools. Does anything about them irritate you?

How could you avoid people thinking the same about your school website?

Keeping records

Be organised

We tend to think of ICT as rules-based and systematic, and we perhaps assume that ICT co-ordinators will be fantastically organised people with a place for everything and highly developed time-management skills. Some are. However, some are the opposite — it is as though their engagement with ICT is a sort of compensation for their personal disorganisation.

Keep files and records of all aspects of your role

Keep these on your computer if you wish, as far as the Data Protection Act permits, but also keep paper-based copies of all key documents and records. You should know, or be able to lay hands on quickly and easily:

- *details of all computer hardware*, including supplier, make, model, serial number, date of purchase and installation, warranty arrangements, service and repair record, technical specification (e.g. processor speed, RAM, hard disk capacity, any upgrades);

- *details of peripheral equipment*, e.g. printers, scanners, digital cameras, floor robots, with information about disposables like ink cartridges or toner;

- *details of all software owned by the school*, including supplier, site licences and multi-user licences, location (e.g. installed on network, available in ICT room, single stand-alone CD-ROM), classes or year groups for which it is intended. You will find it much easier to agree a coherent policy if you establish this, but:

  - don't be rigid about it;
  - don't impose artificial ceilings on children's experience — always remember, many children have access to more sophisticated software at home than you have in your school;
  - don't fall into the trap of assuming that you must always structure software progression through the school in terms of moving on to 'harder' software. There is more virtue in using 'simple' software to the full than there is in skating over the surface of 'harder' software;
  - judge software by its fitness for purpose and pedagogic value in the context in which it is to be used. For example, one can make out a case for needing an 'educational' word processor (e.g. TextEase) *and* an 'industry standard' word processor (e.g. Word) available in every classroom, particularly if teachers have the capacity to use ICT for whole-class teaching. Their functions are rather different — see also Chapter 7;

- *details of web-based resources* in common use in the school — as described above. Obviously, if your school subscribes to any web-based resources which require an annual fee, you must keep a note of that, and preferably a diary showing when fees are due;

- *details of units of work* and short-term and/or long-term plans for teaching ICT as a subject, for each year in the school. This should go beyond simply regurgitating the QCA Scheme of Work for ICT. You, or the school staff collectively, might decide that this is fairly firm ground on which to base your teaching, but try to discourage colleagues from thinking of it as the be-all and end-all. It is not. There are other things that are well worth doing, and new possibilities, with new technologies or new adaptations of existing technologies, regularly present themselves;

- *details of staff training undertaken,* including in-school training days, staff meetings dedicated to ICT, external courses and anything else that might be relevant. Bear in mind that all teachers should have undergone NOF training, or, in the case of newly qualified teachers, have met the same standards during their training courses.

Much of this information should also find its way into the ICT handbook, if you decide to construct one (see Chapters 4 and 5).

Summary

- You need to keep yourself up to date with regard to recent developments in ICT, particularly relating to internet resources.

- Make sure you are well informed about new products, e.g. by visiting the BETT exhibition.

- Check carefully to ensure that your ICT facilities comply with health and safety regulations and recommendations.

- Good initial design and delegation of responsibility are the keys to running a successful school website.

- Be meticulous in the keeping of records.

4 THE ICT POLICY AND DEVELOPMENT PLAN

(→) According to the National Standards for Subject Leadership, you should:

- have knowledge and understanding of the school's aims, priorities, targets and action plans;
- analyse and interpret relevant national, local and school data, research and inspection evidence, to inform policies, practices, expectations, targets and teaching methods;
- establish, with the involvement of relevant staff, short-, medium- and long-term plans for the development and resourcing of the subject which:
  - contribute to whole-school aims, policies and practices including those in relation to behaviour, discipline, bullying and racial harassment;
  - are based on a range of comparative information and evidence, including the attainment of pupils;
  - identify realistic and challenging targets for improvement;
  - are understood by all those involved in putting plans into practice;
  - are clear about action to be taken, timescales and criteria for success;
- have knowledge and understanding of the relationship of the subject to the curriculum as a whole;
- develop and implement policies and practices for the subject which reflect the school's commitment to high achievement, effective teaching and learning;
- ensure that the headteacher, senior managers and governors are well informed about subject policies, plans and priorities, the success in meeting objectives and targets, and subject-related professional development plans.

Background

Every school should have an ICT policy and an ICT development plan. There is also a good case to be made for having a school ICT handbook. Currently the way in which the policy and the plan relate to each other is slightly ambiguous.

According to BECTa,[12] an ICT policy:

> sets out how you use ICT in teaching, learning and the wider context of the school. It should reflect the aims and values of the school, articulate the contribution which ICT makes to pupils' learning, and describe how ICT is used on a day-to-day basis.

An ICT development plan:

> should show what actions you're taking, and what you intend to do, to fulfil your ICT policy.

Your ICT development plan has another function: it will need to be submitted to, and agreed by, your LEA in order to release National Grid for Learning (NGfL) money for ICT resources from the DfES Standards Fund. Without this, you would not be able to afford to improve the provision of hardware in your school.

Ultimately, both documents are the responsibility of the school governors, and neither document can really be completed without significant input from, and a sense of ownership by, the head teacher and the senior management team. However, they would be unwise to complete them without consulting you closely, particularly as you will necessarily bear responsibility for monitoring the implementation of a large part of them. In order to function effectively in your role, you too must feel a sense of ownership of both documents. As we have seen, most ICT co-ordinator job descriptions say or imply that you are responsible for writing the policy document.

Start with a vision of what the place of ICT in your school should be. This should not be your vision alone; it might be the vision of the head teacher or someone else. In a happy situation there will be little difference between your view and that of your head teacher, senior colleagues and governors. There is plenty of evidence that ICT works most effectively when that vision is shared and not merely delegated to you.

The ICT policy

There will already be an ICT policy in your school. You are in luck if is either very good or very bad. If it is very good, perhaps all you will need to do is keep it under review and modify it in the light of developments. If it is very bad, that probably gives you licence to reconstruct it the way you want it to be. Either way, you need to understand something about the history of ICT use in the school, and how that policy was arrived at, and treat the work of your predecessors in the role with a certain amount of sensitivity. Sometimes the reasons why some policy decisions were made only become apparent to you long after you have modified or overturned them.

Whatever state the existing policy is in, you will need to develop your sense of ownership and know it intimately, and the best way to do that is to rewrite it. Bear in mind that you are not the only one who owns it, and that it is one policy among many within the overall development plan of the school. To make your ICT policy effective, you should be familiar with the other relevant documents, including your school's policies on, for example, assessment, special needs and equal opportunities.

The ICT policy needs constant revision and amendment, on at least an annual basis (probably more often than other subjects because of the speed of change), though you do not need to start from scratch each time. If the shape and general philosophy of the policy is well designed, most of your ongoing work will be amendment, revision and updating.

Policy is what you do, not what you write down. It is comparatively common to find schools with carefully constructed documents, complete with rationale and sound pedagogical principles, etc., but actual classroom practice substantially at odds with those principles. As you become acclimatised to the school and to your role within it, try to couch policy in terms that are demanding but manageable. There is no point in setting your colleagues impossibly idealistic goals that they cannot achieve – if all goes well, you can always ratchet it up a bit next year.

- Policy only works if it is well supported by the senior management team.
- Policy only works well if all those people who are going to implement it, including teachers, classroom assistants and any technician support you may have, feel a sense of ownership, and feel that their voices have been heard, their perceived needs met.
- It is perfectly possible to write extremely long and detailed policy documents that nobody takes much notice of, in which case you have wasted your time. Err on the side of brevity.
- Write your policy in everyday language, avoiding unnecessary jargon.

What is the ICT policy for, and what should it contain?

According to BECTa:[21]

> A whole school ICT policy sets out aims and objectives for the teaching and use of ICT in the school. It offers clear guidance on the measures that need to be in place if the requirements of the policy are to be met.

NAACE [58] lists the functions of the school ICT policy as:

- to ensure all staff understand and agree on the approach to ICT;
- to assist planning and promote development;
- to explain the school's position to outsiders;
- to assist the governors in the allocation of funds.

There are no hard-and-fast rules for what must be in your policy or what order you should put things in, though there is no shortage of advice on the subject. Ultimately, you should write the policy that most exactly suits the purposes of your school. If you are seeking advice, there is plenty available if you search the web. Start with the information available from BECTa and NAACE (as above), both of which sites contain detailed and authoritative information. Many LEAs (perhaps including yours) also provide advice, which may be based on at least one of the above, and some also offer templates.

If you have a template available to you, by all means use it to give you structure, and as a way of ensuring you do not omit major areas – as people say (far too often), there is no point in reinventing the wheel – but always keep the specific circumstance of your school firmly in your mind, and adapt the template as appropriate. Some school policies are little more than a slavish regurgitation of a template policy kindly provided by the LEA or another agency. Frankly, this is likely to be an indication of a lack of collective confidence in ICT within the school, and such policies are relatively unlikely to relate directly to what actually gets done.

Do not take the list that follows as definitive or exhaustive – there are plenty of possible variations in the order of things, and different opinions about the level of detail you should include.

- If the school has an agreed vision for the future of ICT, it would be a good idea to begin by articulating that briefly, perhaps as an epigraph. You should make reference to shared beliefs about how ICT can transform the way the school functions.

- There should be a short statement outlining what is meant by the term ICT in the context of your school, and what its scope and significance might be. You might include here reference to the idea that ICT is both a National Curriculum subject and a cross-curricular tool.

- State your overall aims as succinctly as possible. This might be supported by some focused objectives, though these should not merely reproduce what is in the ICT development plan.

- Clarify and justify those aims in terms of factors that might influence them (e.g. National Curriculum requirements, feedback from OFSTED inspections).

- Explain how the school will meet the requirements of the ICT National Curriculum for Key Stages 1 and 2, and, if appropriate, what ICT experiences you would expect children to have in the Foundation Stage, and how this will address the Early Learning Goals. By all means refer in general terms to the QCA Scheme of Work, or any other scheme in use, but do not reproduce it in detail here. If you plan to teach ICT as a generic subject, you might include details of how much time should be devoted to it per week.

- Make a statement about how ICT will be used, and ICT capability developed, in the teaching of all subjects. This, and/or the previous section, might include reference to teaching styles, grouping, etc.

- Outline the roles and responsibilities of the ICT co-ordinator, the teaching staff and the support staff, including reference to any tasks that have been specifically delegated.

- Briefly summarise the ICT resources available, in terms of the deployment of hardware, peripheral equipment and software, particularly with reference to what is allocated to different year groups and what resources are held in common. If there is, for example, a set allocation of time for use of the computer room, explain what it is – but don't include the timetable.

- Supplement this with information about any equipment you may have on open access for children or staff to use on an ad hoc basis (e.g. in the library), and whatever provision you have for the use of equipment outside normal teaching hours.

- Include a brief statement about health and safety in the use of ICT resources, listing the principal areas that need to be considered, with reference to a source (e.g. the ICT handbook or subsection of the overall school health and safety policy statement) in which further details can be found. This section, or the one above, might include reference to internet safety, including any filtering system you may be using, and also the Acceptable Use policy – though this should be produced separately. You might consider it wise to state plainly in the ICT policy that no child will be granted access to the network or the internet unless the Acceptable Use policy has been signed, either by them or on their behalf.

- Refer to whatever the policy is for staff development and training, including how individual staff needs are identified and how progress is monitored.

- Describe how planning and teaching are monitored, and how and when curriculum content will be reviewed and updated.

- Describe any technical support you have available.

- Relate the ICT policy to other policies, e.g. equal opportunities, special needs.

- State clearly how ICT will be used to foster inclusion and support the specific needs of pupils.

- Include a statement acknowledging that many children make extensive use of ICT outside school, and explaining how that will affect the way ICT is used in school.

- Explain how the use of ICT will be assessed, recorded and reported, including any arrangements for moderation of standards between classes, years and key stages, or the maintenance of a school portfolio. If pupils are expected to engage in self-assessment, include reference to this.

- Make reference to policy in the use of ICT for administration purposes (even though this is not your responsibility).

- Make a statement about policy in relation to the possible use of school ICT facilities by parents and the local community.

- Refer briefly to other legal or ethical issues, including licensing, copyright and data protection.

- Include the date on which the policy was formally adopted, and identify a future date by which it will be updated. Some people see a policy statement as having validity for five years; given the speed of technological innovation, this may be over generous. Aim to review and tweak it every year, and perhaps overhaul it every three years.

There are many more points that might be included, but your aim is to produce a practically useful document that will stand as an adequate and accurate record of how things are done in your school, and that will not be turgid and unreadable.

Who are the stakeholders?

Who might read your ICT policy?

- Firstly, you will. It should become very familiar to you. That level of familiarity, though essential, carries with it certain small dangers. It is easy to take some key points for granted, or, because they have been so much in your mind, to inadvertently neglect to commit them to paper. It is useful to have a critical friend (see below).

- New members of staff will read it. According to BECTa,[21] they will use the policy to:

  - *understand the school's approach to the teaching and use of ICT;*
  - *obtain guidance in the way they should be using ICT in their lessons;*
  - *find out what support may be available to develop further their ICT skills, knowledge and capabilities.*

- Your teaching colleagues will read it. When they read it, they will be thinking in terms of the things it commits them to do. For that policy to have any credibility as a statement about what they actually do, they must have some sense of ownership of it, and they must consider its aims to be achievable. BECTa[21] suggests that existing teachers will use the policy to:

  - *gauge what access they should have to ICT facilities and equipment;*
  - *assess future ICT developments and their impact on their work;*
  - *learn how other year group teachers are using ICT, helping their cross-curricular planning;*
  - *understand the responsibilities involved in the teaching and use of ICT;*
  - *offer guidance on the extent to which ICT should be incorporated into their individual lessons and subject schemes of work;*
  - *know what procedures exist to monitor and assess pupils' ICT capability.*

  This is a rather daunting list, but not overwhelming if you accept that some of these purposes can be met, not within the policy document itself, but in an ICT handbook (see below).

- The head teacher and senior management team will read it, and will probably contribute to the writing of it. They should be considering it in the light of the overall school development plan, and considering how it meshes in with all the other policies in operation. They will probably also consider it in terms of resource implications – how much will it cost to maintain this policy, and what expenditure it commits the school to in the short, medium and long term.

- The school governors will read it. If you are invited to the governors' meeting (or curriculum subcommittee meeting) where it is discussed and approved, bear in mind that it is the function of school governing bodies to be supportive and friendly, but also objective and constructively critical. Though some school governors are education professionals in one sense or another, many are not. The chances are that at least one governor will be a person who makes extensive use of information technology in a non-educational context, e.g. in an office. Make sure the educational logic of your policy is well to the fore.

- BECTa suggests that non-teaching curriculum support staff will also read it, to ascertain the level of ICT provision that may be available to support individual learners, to find out where responsibilities lie, e.g. for installing software, and to find information about future plans. Again, some of this information may be better placed in an ICT handbook.

- Parents and prospective parents are entitled to read it. According to BECTA[21] they may do so in order to:

  - *find out what ICT experiences their children should have at school;*
  - *help them to decide how to support their child's learning with ICT;*
  - *compare the provision and approach of different schools.*

- LEA advisory staff may well read it. Bear in mind that they will also have read many other ICT policies, and may be able to offer you good advice in the writing of it.

- OFSTED inspectors will certainly read it. This is a good reason for ensuring that it is realistic and bears a resemblance to actual practice, but is forward looking and examines ways in which ICT can or should develop.

- If you put your policies on your school website, as some schools do, anyone in the world can read it. Just as you may have looked at some other policies when constructing yours, let yours be a shining example to others.

How should you go about writing an ICT policy?

- Firstly, consult. Talk to as many of the identified stakeholders as you can.

- Examine examples of existing policies.

- Reread the present school policy.

- Draft a new version of the policy. If you get stuck on the wording of a section, leave it, and go on to the next section – very often, doing so will help you to see what you need to write.

- Think about the internal logic of what you have written. Does each point seem to follow on naturally from the last?

- Engage the help of a critical friend who knows relatively little about primary schools and primary ICT. What does your friend think of it? If you find yourself having to explain things, consider what the implications of that are, and make whatever revisions you think are necessary.

- Present your policy document at a staff meeting, as a draft for discussion and further amendment. Try not to let it be the last agenda item. Listen to what your colleagues have to say; you will almost certainly have left out something that someone else thinks is vital.

- Act upon suggestions given – remember that the goal is embedded practice and a sense of shared ownership.

Reflection

Using the internet, locate and print out the ICT policies of at least four schools from totally different parts of the country. Read them all carefully and compare them.

- *What do they have in common?*

- *In what ways do they differ from each other?*

- *Do some feel too short to say anything useful?*

- *Are some so verbose that they are a struggle to read?*

- *When you read each one, how much do you feel you actually know about how ICT is used in that school -- not in specific details, but in terms of underlying principles or ethos? What can you learn from this?*

- *Can you identify things that you would definitely have done or expressed differently?*

- *What good ideas or useful turns of phrase can you filch from them?*

The ICT development plan

If you are new to the profession, or have not yet qualified, you may find what follows a little daunting. Do not worry. This is very much the business of senior management within the school, and in some respects it can be thought of as a subset of the overall school development plan. Nobody should expect you to take overall responsibility for this. It is included here because you should be consulted about it, and your day-to-day management of your role will be affected by it.

What follows is a summary of the BECTa advice sheet, *What Makes a Good ICT Development Plan?*[28] The underlying principles are the same, whether you work in a 30-child rural primary school or a 2,500-student comprehensive school.

The ICT development plan should address how the school will:

- maintain and develop the infrastructure of hardware and connectivity in a way that is sustainable without distracting teachers from their teaching;

- ensure that the infrastructure enables staff to access valuable content (in terms of resources and tools);

- develop and sustain practice, including ongoing training and curriculum development.

The plan should be:

- credible;

- manageable;

- sustainable.

It should address

- philosophy and aims;
- curriculum aspects;
- management of ICT;
- professional development of teachers and other staff;
- hardware and deployment;
- financial aspects;
- monitoring and review;
- planning needs.

As you can see, as ICT co-ordinator much of this will be your business.

Four elements in the process of developing the ICT development plan are:

- the ICT audit – establishing where you are now;
- aims and objectives – deciding where you want to be by agreeing a vision and setting targets;
- the implementation plan – an action plan to achieve those aims;
- evaluation – monitoring progress to see if the aims are being achieved.

The ICT audit

The ICT audit is intended to address the question *where are we now?* Even if there was no such thing as the ICT development plan, you would probably wish to conduct an audit for your own purposes in order to set your own priorities. You are likely to be involved in the data-gathering exercise and will certainly want to use the resulting information to underpin your work. In examining current provision these are some of the points you will need to consider.

- Teaching and learning of ICT as a subject and as a cross-curricular tool:
  - Does the current teaching of ICT as a subject ensure that the whole of the Programme of Study is being covered adequately?
  - Is this true for all children?
  - Is there evidence of continuity and progression in the way ICT is planned for and taught?
  - Are the needs of all children being met, including the very able, those with identified special educational needs, and those who have substantial experience with ICT, or no experience, outside the school?
  - Is ICT used effectively to support, enhance or transform teaching and learning across the curriculum as a whole?
  - To what extent is this true in all subjects and in all classes?
  - Does the use of ICT make a significant contribution to the Literacy Hour and the

daily mathematics lesson?

- Is ICT being used to enable children with special needs to access the curriculum?
- Does current practice in lesson planning pay sufficient attention to the possibilities afforded by ICT?
- Where the use of ICT is planned, is it actually delivered?

- Resources, including hardware, software and peripheral equipment:

  - Do you have enough computers to meet your needs, or to reach the ratio expected?
  - Are your computers sufficiently up to date and powerful to enable you to meet the demands that will be placed upon them?
  - Are your computers deployed in the best possible locations to ensure effective use?
  - Are you meeting the needs of children who require adapted equipment or special access devices?
  - Do you have enough printers, cameras, interactive whiteboards, etc. to meet your needs?
  - Do you have enough equipment to undertake relatively specialised tasks like datalogging or control?
  - Is the software available to you appropriate for the purposes to which it will be put, and suitable for the age of the children who will be using it?
  - Do you have a sufficient range of software to support the use of ICT appropriately across the whole curriculum?

- The current level of staff awareness and competence:

  - Have all staff completed NOF training, or its equivalent?
  - Are there mechanisms in place for identifying specific staff training needs?
  - Is there adequate opportunity for staff development?

- Procedures for monitoring and assessment:

  - Is there an effective strategy for monitoring and evaluating the use of ICT throughout the school?
  - Do teachers have effective means of monitoring children's progress and achievement, both in ICT as a subject and in the use of ICT in other subjects?
  - Are teachers' assessments of children's capabilities in line with National Curriculum expectations?
  - Does the school maintain an ICT portfolio, identifying expected standards for each National Curriculum level?

- How ICT is viewed in the school, by teachers, children, and everyone else:

  - Is there a general expectation in the school that the use of ICT will have a beneficial effect on children's education?
  - Do teachers view the use of ICT in subjects as a key skill?
  - Is the level of acceptance and use of ICT uniformly appropriate throughout the school, or is it patchy?
  - Do all members of staff make effective use of ICT for their own purposes, e.g. in planning, record keeping or resource preparation?

- Is there evidence that parents, governors and other outside parties are broadly interested in, and supportive of, the use of ICT in the school?

- How ICT is funded:
  - Including Standards Fund money, is there sufficient money provided to enable the provision of ICT resources to move forwards?
  - Are there long-, medium- and short-term plans for the provision of new resources?
  - Is there a coherent and manageable strategy for the replacement of older equipment?

You could no doubt construct a much longer and more detailed list, but you need to ensure that the process remains manageable. It would pre-empt and largely duplicate the rest of this book to look at each of these in greater detail here.

It would be a mammoth task to try to collect information to support all the questions listed above. Be selective — the process will need to be repeated in subsequent years, and you can build up a composite picture over time. Try not to persecute your colleagues with highly elaborate questionnaires. Much of the information you seek can be gleaned from self-assessment by teachers, by informal discussion or by your own observations. BECTa[13] recommends that an audit by walking around (ABWA) can provide you with a useful snapshot of how things are at the present time. Chapter 7 includes more suggestions for conducting the hardware audit.

Aims and objectives

Your ICT development plan should be devised in the light of the picture that emerges from the audit of the state of ICT in your school. The school should identify what its priorities are, and identify and agree clear aims and objectives which should relate to the school's vision for ICT. Everything on the plan should:

- have a timescale;
- be costed;
- state who is responsible for seeing that objectives are met (in many cases this is likely to be you);
- include provision for evaluation.

Targets should be SMART, that is:

- Specific.
- Measurable.
- Achievable.
- Realistic.
- Timed.

Your LEA may well produce a framework or matrix to assist you in the process of completing this task. Remember that it is not your job to do it, but you should be consulted over the process.

What the ICT development plan should include

Guidance from the DfES,[8][5] identifies the areas to be covered in the plan. For primary schools in 2002–3, these include:

- how the school will use ICT to help raise educational standards by enhancing the delivery of the National Curriculum;

- how ICT will contribute to the achievement of targets set by the school for improvements in the number of children achieving level four and above in mathematics and English and what use will be made of guidance from the National Numeracy and Literacy Strategy on using ICT to teach more effectively;

- how investment in ICT will be co-ordinated with meeting the professional development needs of its teachers, including through the take-up of training opportunities funded by the New Opportunities Fund (NOF);

- how the school's ICT facilities will be made available for use out of normal school hours by pupils and for community purposes;

- how ICT will be used to promote inclusion, for example by supporting pupils with special educational needs and by developing home–school links (including the development of a school website);

- the school's policy for the acceptable use of ICT, including the use of e-mail and the internet;

- an audit of levels of equipping, network use and teacher development currently being undertaken;

- setting out the school's policy for managing, developing and sustaining its ICT provision, including accommodation/access issues;

- arrangements for technical support;

- the safe and environmentally friendly disposal of equipment.

In order for NGfL funds to be released, schools are required to record that they have committed themselves to achieving the pupil:computer ratio specified by the DfES. In primary schools for 2002 this was 11:1. For 2004 the figure is 8:1.

There are also areas of the plan relating to the use of ICT for school management and administration purposes, but these are not your responsibility. There is an expectation that this plan will be made freely available to the public, for example through your school website.

Several of the areas identified above will be addressed in the chapters that follow.

The ICT handbook

Though it does not yet appear to be a widespread practice in primary schools, you should consider creating a school ICT handbook. According to NAACE:[58]

> It is common for a school ICT policy to have the main messages swamped by rules and procedural issues. Procedures, guidance, rules and other operational matters should be placed in a handbook.

Freedman (1999)[48] suggests that a handbook will provide useful evidence when you are inspected; certainly, it is a way of gathering much pertinent information together in one place. It could exist in a number of formats – perhaps, if your older colleagues can bear it, as a ring binder. Certainly, you should store as much of the information as possible in electronic format so that it can be updated quickly and easily. You might include:

- a statement of the school's vision for ICT;
- a copy of the ICT policy;
- a copy of the ICT development plan;
- details of the deployment of hardware;
- lists of software in common use in different classes or years;
- a guide to ICT terminology – you might include a glossary and a list of abbreviations for reference;
- a detailed guide to equipment and procedures in the computer room;
- brief guides to support the use of large equipment like interactive whiteboards and peripheral equipment like digital cameras;
- if you have a large number of identical computers deployed around the school, it might be worth your while to include a diagram of where things plug in, and so forth;
- summaries of the National Curriculum Programmes of Study for ICT and copies of level descriptions;
- details of the scheme(s) of work being followed. This would be the place to identify which QCA units (or whatever) are being addressed by which classes during which term. This should help to keep colleagues informed about continuity and progression, and should, in theory at least, reduce the incidence of several classes wanting access to the same scarce resources at the same time;
- a copy of the rules for the use of the computer room;
- a copy of the school's Acceptable Use policy;
- information about health and safety considerations when ICT is being used;
- photocopiable sheets (or, more usefully, template files) of basic record-keeping forms;
- details of school procedures – how to book equipment, how to report equipment failure, etc.

Reflection

Can you think of anything important that is missing from the above list?

You will probably find it desirable to arrange the handbook in different sections and include a table of contents at the front. Keep its appearance bright and cheerful (this is often achieved by the use of a few well-chosen graphics and the Comic Sans font), and do not overburden colleagues with huge wodges of continuous prose but make extensive use of subheadings and bullet points. Store it electronically, and update it and reprint altered sections at least annually. If you have an intranet, and a penchant for such things, you might consider turning it into a set of web pages, with hyperlinked cross-references.

It is entirely up to you how many paper copies of the handbook you actually produce – certainly one for yourself, one for the head teacher, one for OFSTED, then perhaps one staffroom copy, or one per department, or one for each teacher and teaching assistant. Ask colleagues what else they would like it to include. For more suggestions, see Chapter 5.

Summary

Your school ICT policy and ICT development plan are significant documents for which everyone should have a sense of ownership. Policy should be expressed in manageable terms, and should relate to what you actually do. The ICT development plan should be based upon an audit of ICT resources and skills, and should set out SMART objectives for moving the school forwards. An ICT handbook is a useful way of collating all the important information about ICT for the benefit of colleagues.

5 WORKING WITH OTHERS – STAFF DEVELOPMENT

(→) According to the National Standards for Subject Leadership, you should:

- set expectations and targets for staff and pupils in relation to standards of pupil achievement and the quality of teaching;

- ensure curriculum coverage, continuity and progression in the subject for all pupils, including those of high ability and those with special educational or linguistic needs;

- establish clear expectations and constructive working relationships among staff, including through team working and mutual support; devolving responsibilities and delegating tasks, appropriate evaluating practice; and developing an acceptance of accountability;

- lead professional development through example and support, and co-ordinate the provision of high-quality professional development by methods such as coaching, drawing on other sources of expertise as necessary, for example higher education, LEAs and subject associations;

- ensure that trainee and newly qualified teachers are appropriately trained, monitored, supported and assessed in relation to standards for the award of Qualified Teacher Status, the Career Entry Profiles and standards for induction;

- create a climate which enables other staff to develop and maintain positive attitudes towards the subject and confidence in teaching it.

In considering ways in which people adopt technological change, Rogers (1995)[76] suggests that the distribution is approximately:

- *Innovators* – adventurous, who have financial resources and like to play with new tools (5 per cent);

- *Early Adopters* – those who see strategic advantage in adopting an innovation (10 per cent);

- *Early Majority* – followers who make a deliberate choice to adopt (35 per cent);

- *Late Majority* – those who are sceptical and who adopt when it is less risky (35 per cent);

- *Laggards* – those who adopt a 'not over my dead body' attitude (15 per cent);

Almost by definition, primary ICT co-ordinators tend to fit into either the first or second of these categories (perhaps mostly the second). The majority of teachers, however, do not. According to McKenzie[55] (based on Moore, 1991[56]), at least 70 per cent of teachers fall into the 'reluctant' or 'late adopter' categories. This has consequences for the way in which ICT has developed in primary schools. A potential problem is that the assumption that late adopters will eventually follow the lead of early adopters is not necessarily true. McKenzie lists some key characteristics of late adopters.

- *Late adopters want proof of results before they buy.*
  - One of the most important differences Moore identifies between the two groups is the expectation of late adopters that new technologies must make a very big difference in outcomes and performance. They have little tolerance for change and are unwilling to shift time tested behaviours unless there is compelling evidence that the investment of time and effort will pay big dividends.

- *Late adopters want a complete, finished product before they buy.*
  - They also expect a complete package, a total solution that is user friendly, complete and well supported. They are, in Moore's terms, pragmatists. They are conservative and distrustful of change for change sake. They have their eye on the bottom line. They have no patience for half-baked ideas, unproven technologies and untested schemes.

McKenzie lists nine strategies for reaching late adopters and reluctant technology users. These are, briefly:

- demonstrate real gains in student performance when ICT is used;
- deliver a complete package – they do not have time to 'mess around' with things that are still under development;
- eliminate risk and surprise;
- speak their language;
- offer continual support;
- emphasise teams – aim staff development at groups of teachers working as a team;
- find out what turns them on;
- provide rewards and incentives;
- don't rely on pioneers alone to plan for reluctants.

Of course, things have moved on substantially in the last few years. Most teachers (87 per cent in 2002)[37] have access to their own computer. Thousands of teachers have benefited so far from the 'Laptops for Teachers' scheme, which extends at least until 2006.[63] By the completion of the process in 2003, all teachers should have undergone the New Opportunities Fund (NOF) training scheme, which spent £230 million on attempting to bring teachers to a point where they could make effective use of ICT in the teaching of core subjects, at least. For a view on the extent to which this process was successful, see in particular OFSTED (2002) pages 22–4.[68]

Reflection

Do you agree with McKenzie's view about early and late adopters?

Of the teachers you know and have worked with, what proportion would you say fell into each category?

What are the consequences of this for you as an ICT co-ordinator?

Informal help and advice

As indicated in Chapter 2, you will be asked for advice and practical help, sometimes at very inconvenient moments. It is worth developing goodwill, but if you revel in the role of the One Who Knows and make yourself indispensable, your job will get harder and you will leave a vacuum when you move on. Think of the informal help you give as part of a long-term strategy to shift people's basic assumptions.

The first step in good staff development is to set a good example yourself, and without evangelising or boring, let other members of staff see some of the benefits that accrue from effective ICT use, especially in terms of your personal organisation. Make sure your own teaching materials are well-produced, you find information on the internet quickly and efficiently by means of intelligent searching, and your class make frequent and valuable use of ICT to support their learning – but don't hog the equipment. If you attend a training session, share the outcomes informally with colleagues.

The next step is to delegate parts of your role. You may be able to do some of this formally, through the ICT policy. Get other people to have a look at new software for you, and ask them to be the ones to report back to other colleagues. When there is an opportunity to go on a specific training session (particularly if it is about something you think you already know), get someone else to go. You are trying to create an ethos in which ICT use is embedded as a natural part of what everybody does, both in their classrooms and outside.

Motivating reluctant colleagues

You are unlikely to encounter any teachers who absolutely refuse to make use of ICT in their teaching, because it is well established that children have a statutory right to it, OFSTED will expect to find it, and some parents will certainly notice if it is not happening. All teachers should have undergone NOF training. This is not to say, of course, that all your colleagues will be equally enthusiastic about it. There is a litany of excuses that reluctant teachers have tended to trot out, some of which are based on previous negative experiences:

- *My computer/disk drive/monitor/printer is broken.*
  Over the years, school computer equipment has tended to go wrong far too often. This might be partly a result of the pouring of drinks over the keyboard or

the posting of biscuits into the disk drive or other mistreatment by grubby little fingers. On the other hand, sometimes the fault is extremely minor and can be fixed in a few moments – but some teachers have been known to use this excuse for months on end, which suggests that the real problem lies elsewhere.

- *Every time I have tried to use a computer, something has gone wrong.*
  There is a cycle at work – ICT competence leads to confidence, which leads to greater competence, and so on. Some teachers have difficulty mounting this cycle, and when they do, the chain comes off, and there is an understandable lack of forward momentum. If you are not confident to start with, you tend to look at problems as excuses for inaction rather than challenges to be met.

- *I have so much else to do that I don't have time to learn the software.*
  Teachers are extremely busy people, and it is sometimes difficult to persuade them to make an initial investment of time, even though it should pay dividends in the future. This excuse is perhaps the principal reason why so many teachers have adopted an attitude to ICT that amounts to putting a supposedly educational game on the classroom computer and telling the children, in effect, 'Go over there and get on with that, and don't bother me with it.' Most of the time, of course, the process of 'learning the software', at least to a basic working level, can be accomplished in a few minutes, particularly if it is done alongside a collea-gue who already knows what it does and what its most useful features are. The rapid increase in the number of teachers who have access to a computer at home has meant that a much higher proportion of teachers now use computers to help them with their lesson preparations, and those who still create all their resources by hand must notice that they are often at a disadvantage. However, do not tell anyone that computers will save them time – they conspicuously do not do that.

- *Children should be engaged in practical activity, not sitting passively staring at a screen.*
  This is a point of view often expressed by Early Years teachers, which finds its most eloquent expression in the Alliance for Childhood report, *Fool's Gold*[2] – see also Chapter 6. No teacher will deny the truth of the first part of the state-ment, but there are two main objections to the second part. Firstly, it is not an either/or situation; children should have time to do both – though as a general principal, you should avoid using software that reproduces on screen an activity could have been done at least as well in real life. Secondly, although children may not be physically moving about, making effective use of a computer is never a passive process.

Reflection

What other excuses have you encountered for not using ICT?

How would you rebut them?

Where an opening presents itself for you to support and help a reluctant colleague, try to hold any initial discussions in their classroom rather than in the staffroom, the ICT suite or your room. At an unconscious level, territory is sometimes an important factor. Have a look at their walls, their books, their classroom layout, and try to form an impression of their priorities and the things that really matter to them. Try to identify ways in which ICT can help them with the things they really like doing. Very often these opportunities arise when you are asked to sort out a minor glitch in a classroom computer – if so (assuming you can solve the problem), don't leave the conversation there:

Ah, needlepoint! I like these. I came across a really good website the other day, with lots of free needlepoint patterns, suitable for children to do. Would it be helpful to you if I passed you the address?

Devious and Machiavellian, perhaps, but it works. If you *are* interested in needlepoint websites, try Aion.[1]

Reflection

Can you think of any other devious ways to enthuse reluctant colleagues?
What is important is to develop their sense of ownership, and sometimes the sense that they are, in their own way, the Ones Who Know about a particular aspect of ICT, however small or localised that might be.

Making and maintaining lists of web addresses

If, as suggested in Chapter 3, you have been gathering a long list of potentially useful websites, make this available to colleagues, with the URLs and a brief description of what the site is for, what parts you think might be particularly useful and what pitfalls, if any, you have discovered. Organise your list by year group, by subject and theme, or better still both. Provide a paper handout, but also make it available in electronic form, as a word processor file or even a web page, so that colleagues can click on URLs and go straight to sites. It is very offputting for timid users to keep encountering the screen that says 'The page cannot be displayed', because they have made a simple typing error. Similarly, if you are updating lists you have previously created, take a few minutes to check that links still work – there is absolutely no guarantee that they will do so year after year. Head your list with a phrase like 'All sites accessed 03/03/03'. Let it be known among colleagues that you are interested in hearing from them of any other potentially useful sites they have found – preferably, persuade them to e-mail you the URL. Make a point of trying to incorporate colleagues' suggestions in your list promptly, and thank them publicly for their suggestions – remember that your goal should be a sense of shared ownership.

Staff meetings

It is probably a good idea to convince your head teacher to make ICT issues a permanent agenda item for staff meetings. On some occasions there may be little to say, of course. Remember, though, that ICT is just an agenda item, and not the reason the staff meeting was called. Obviously, if you are setting up a new computer room, or re-writing the ICT policy, it might be a major item. Use the staff meeting as an opportunity to tell colleagues about:

- new and intended purchases;
- forthcoming courses and events;
- the current state of hardware, software and peripheral equipment;
- minor changes in policy or strategy.

Also use the staff meeting to ask colleagues about issues in ICT that concern them, though you will probably be stopped from letting this turn into a technical discussion about how to use mail merge in Word. Offer to have those discussions outside the meeting, and suggest that anyone else who wishes to participate should also join in.

Organising a staff development day

Inevitably, it will fall to your lot to organise staff development days for ICT.

- Aim to spend not less than one day per year on staff ICT development. There is much to be said for setting up two half days rather than a whole day, so that colleagues do not feel they are suffering from information overload.
- Given the choice, opt for a morning session – you might want to carry on talking about what you did over lunch, and nobody should be in a hurry to rush off at the end of your session.
- Your first task might be to convince the head teacher that you need at least two half days per year. With the seemingly ceaseless flow of new initiatives in education, there is never a shortage of things that need to be discussed. Your best way in to that discussion is to emphasise the rapidity with which ICT is developing, the need for everyone to keep up to speed and the kudos that accrues from being a school which is identified as making good use of ICT.
- You should think carefully about who you wish to be at the development day –
  - teachers, obviously;
  - do not let the head teacher back out from attending the whole session – there is ample evidence that ICT works best in schools where the head teacher is actively involved in its promotion and development;
  - classroom assistants, wherever possible;
  - if you are unveiling major new resources, extend an invitation to the governors.
- Decide where you want to hold your meeting. This will often be dictated by obvious factors – you would not dream of sitting in the staffroom talking to people about how to use the new computer room. Don't overlook the obvious,

just because it is obvious – make sure you choose a comfortable space, and don't expect your colleagues to spend the whole morning sitting on infant chairs.

- Make sure coffee and lunch arrangements are properly made – it has been known for each of the organisers of two half-day sessions to assume that the other has arranged lunch!

- Decide well in advance what you wish your programme to include. Ask your colleagues what they would like to include.

- Make sure that any printing you need to have done is ready well before the day.

- Have more than one item on the agenda. You might want to include:
  - demonstrations of new hardware, software or peripheral equipment;
  - hands-on training;
  - discussions relating to the ICT policy, the development plan, the forthcoming OFSTED inspection or whatever;
  - show and tell sessions in which colleagues describe ways in which ICT has worked effectively for their class;
  - outside speakers, perhaps to demonstrate products, or someone from the LEA advisory staff, or possibly the ICT co-ordinator from another nearby primary school (particularly if that school has Beacon status for its ICT).

- Most really worthwhile software has applicability across more than one year group, and it is good policy for teachers to be aware of what is being done in the years above and below the one in which they currently teach to avoid unnecessary duplication or tackling prematurely something that could be covered to greater effect at a later stage. Many teachers have had the experience of being told by a class, 'We did this last year', and discovering that the topic in hand was previously covered too superficially to have been really effective in developing children's understanding – which actually makes it harder to teach. If the ICT policy is working well, of course, this should not really happen very much – however, the greatest crime in teaching is setting artificial ceilings on children's experience.

- If you have arranged for a demonstration by an outside agency, have an extra agenda item up your sleeve in case unforeseen circumstances cause a last-minute cancellation.

- Build in flexibility, and decide in advance what could be curtailed if necessary – particularly with ICT, things almost always overrun.

- When you hold discussions, bear in mind that at least some of your colleagues will be very reluctant to venture anything in a large group. If you split discussions up into small groups, be absolutely clear about what is to be discussed, what decisions should be reached, what the timing of the discussion is to be, and what groups are supposed to report back at the end. It is often a good idea to set different (but related) tasks to different groups, and ask colleagues to opt for one group or another.

- Always finish with a plenary, in which you can receive feedback and recapitulate the main themes of the morning.

As the ICT co-ordinator you will be expected to hold the proceedings together, and you will do your career no harm if can demonstrate that you can organise a well-orchestrated, efficient, stimulating and productive session. You will be expected to introduce agenda items, facilitate discussions, keep things to time and make summarising remarks. It is at your discretion whether you ask the head teacher (or chair of governors) to make the opening or closing remarks.

Do not underestimate the importance of getting colleagues to talk about and demonstrate things that have worked for them in their classes. Keep such presentations short, but invite questions from the rest of the staff. Do not cajole those who do not wish to be cajoled, but drop in the suggestion that in the fullness of time there is an expectation that everyone will want to present something. Probably the most important part of this exercise is the question time at the end. Try to say as little as possible yourself, and certainly do not lead the conversation into technical areas. Remember that your principal aim is to spread responsibility for ICT as widely as possible, to embed it in everybody's everyday practice.

Another possible agenda item is everyday maintenance and basic good practice. You will certainly want to cover this if you are inducting colleagues into the mysteries of the new ICT room, but it is likely to prove a very popular item at any time. Things that seem very basic and obvious to you do not necessarily appear so to others, and even though everyone should have undergone NOF training, the chances are that there are still simple things that have eluded them – and quite possibly you as well.

Demonstrate and explain those simple things, like:

- what plugs in where;
- how to make effective use of Windows 2000 or XP, or whatever operating system you have;
- what various icons mean;
- how to make efficient use of folders and directories;
- keyboard shortcuts;
- how to format a floppy disk;
- how to improve mouse performance by cleaning the wheels;
- how to fit a printer cartridge;
- how to readjust a monitor if little fingers have twiddled all the knobs;
- how to use a search engine efficiently.

Ask colleagues to list the things that they really want to know and answer them if you can, or else promise to do so at a later date – however well informed you think you are, you will almost certainly be caught out by something you don't know the answer to. The more successfully you conduct this exercise, the fewer of your break-times will be spent in other people's classrooms. In particular, make sure that classroom assistants are party to all of this – increasingly their role will include simple maintenance and setting up of equipment, and a good knowledge of techniques will be a great asset. The contents of these sessions might usefully be summarised in your ICT handbook, if you devise one.

Reflection

Would you want parents to attend your staff training day? Think of reasons why this might be a good idea, and reasons why it might be a bad idea.

Would you consider inviting children to at least part of the training day, to give demonstrations? List the advantages and disadvantages of doing so.

NQTs and students

Newly qualified teachers (NQTs) frequently identify ICT as an area for development on their Career Entry Profiles. Whoever is responsible for mentoring them may well wish to enlist your help in meeting their needs. Bear in mind that every teacher now qualifying must have met the Professional Standards for Qualified Teacher Status,[83] and must have passed the TTA ICT skills test, so no NQT should be an absolute beginner, and in many cases you will probably find that they are well informed and positively motivated, and may already possess skills well in advance of many long-serving teachers. What they may not have, however, is extensive experience of making effective use of ICT in the classroom – this is still, to some extent, the luck of the draw in whatever schools and classes they did their teaching placements. Think of them as your natural allies. Particularly if they are young, everyone else will assume that they will take quite naturally to making good use of ICT in their classrooms. They will almost certainly have access to a computer outside school, and most will be familiar with planning lessons and making resources with ICT.

If your school supports trainees on teaching practice, maintain a watching brief on their use of ICT. In some cases they will have specific requirements placed upon them by their course to undertake some particular ICT activity, and you should know what that activity is intended to be, and whether or not it will be possible for them to do it in the context in which they are placed. Be sensitive to their needs. On occasions you might need to arrange some specific provision of hardware or software to assist them.

Ask your trainees, or the school's lead mentor, to provide you with details of their ICT courses, and particularly with details of assignments. Their university or college should be sensitive to particular hardware and software policies or trends in effect at LEA level, so there should be a high level of harmonisation between the software you have and the software they might expect to find. If there is not, then give serious consideration to some of their expectations when you are revising your list of intended software purchases.

If any trainees are pursuing ICT as a specialist subject or special interest area, they may well wish to talk to you at some length, discuss the ICT policy with you, or perhaps even shadow you on occasions in the discharge of your duties. The chances are that readers of this book have found themselves in exactly that position as trainees. Do what you can to oblige them, but keep in mind always that your absolute first duty is to be a good general teacher of the children in your class. Bear in mind that even ICT specialist trainees are fairly unlikely to gain first-hand experience of network management in their university or college, so if that is one of your roles, that is a worthwhile area in which to be shadowed.

Reflection

If you have already qualified as a teacher: is there anything that the ICT co-ordinator in your placement schools could have done to assist you more?

Or if you are still a trainee, what would really help you?

What lessons can you draw from this about how you might support trainees in future?

Summary

A substantial proportion of teachers are not early adopters of new technology, and need support in order to reach an understanding of how ICT might transform what they do. Your task is to supply this support informally, and also formally through staff meetings and staff development days. Make sure your support extends to NQTs and students.

6 ICT AS A SUBJECT AND AS A CROSS-CURRICULAR RESOURCE

(→) According to the National Standards for Subject Leadership, you should:

- have knowledge and understanding of the characteristics of high quality teaching and the main strategies for improving and sustaining high standards of teaching, learning and achievement for all pupils;
- have knowledge and understanding of the relationship of the subject to the curriculum as a whole.

What makes leadership in ICT more complex than leadership in any other subject is that it is not simply a subject. Those who know about it have grown accustomed to the idea that when we say ICT we mean both the National Curriculum subject of that name and also the cross-curricular tool, the means of enhancing teaching and learning in all subjects. Those who do not know sufficient about it can often lose sight of the difference between the two. For a while the term IT was used to denote the National Curriculum subject, and ICT to denote the technologies used to enhance teaching and learning, but this caused considerable confusion, and both senses are now referred to as ICT. The term ICT was coined by the Stevenson Committee in their report commissioned by the Labour Party (Stevenson, 1997)[78] which has provided a rationale and backdrop for much government policy ever since:

> On a point of definition we talk in this report of ICT, adding 'communications' to the more familiar 'information technology'. This seems to us accurately to reflect the increasing role of both information and communication technologies in all aspects of society.

It is perhaps worth noting the continuing discrepancy in understanding about what the C stands for. Stevenson clearly intended it to stand for *communications* with a final *s*, and this is how it is interpreted by BECTa, among others. OFSTED and QCA have a preference for *communication* without an *s*. DfES sources use either term more or less interchangeably. The QCA Scheme of Work, on the other hand, is still officially for IT. For more details about definitions and distinctions, see BECTa.[27]

ICT at the Foundation Stage

If your school includes children at the Foundation Stage, i.e. in Nursery or Reception classes, you will need to ensure that ICT is appropriately catered for, and that teachers and other adults working in that context have a good understanding of the role that ICT can play.

Most Foundation Stage classrooms have access to a computer, but in some cases it seems that it is turned on for use as a free activity, with the same piece of simple software (often a game intended to develop hand–eye co-ordination) loaded for weeks on end and with little or no direct adult intervention, except occasionally to start children off or to reset the machine when it goes wrong.

In fact, much of the best ICT activity at the Foundation Stage does not involve the use of a computer at all. The *Curriculum Guidance for the Foundation Stage*[73] suggests that teachers should use a whole range of different devices, including televisions, radios, video recorders, photocopiers, digital cameras, music keyboards and a vast array of programmable toys and robots.

The ICT Early Learning Goal within 'Knowledge and understanding of the world' states:[73]

- *find out about and identify the uses of everyday technology and use of information and communication technology and programmable toys to support their learning.*

In order to meet this, the practitioner needs to:

- *give opportunities for the use of ICT to develop skills across the areas of learning, for example a talking word processor to develop language and communication, vocabulary and writing, talking books for early reading, a paint program to develop early mark making, a telephone for speaking and listening, CD-ROMs, video and television and musical tapes to find things out;*
- *encourage children to observe and talk about the use of ICT in the environment on local walks, for example traffic lights, telephones, street lights, barcode scanners to identify prices in shops;*
- *encourage children to show each other how to use ICT equipment.*

The 'Stepping stones' for this state that children should:

- *show an interest in ICT;*
- *know how to operate simple equipment;*
- *complete a simple program on the computer and/or perform simple functions on ICT apparatus.*

For further information and ideas to support the use of ICT in the Foundation Stage, see the VTC[88] and BECTa sites.[26]

ICT in the National Curriculum

Much of what follows relates to the National Curriculum for England. There is separate provision for Wales, Scotland and Northern Ireland. Links can be found to relevant sites from the National Curriculum website.[43]

In the original version of the National Curriculum there was no such subject as ICT (or IT). It existed as a subset of design and technology. There was also reference to the use of computers and software in a number of other subjects (word processing in English, LOGO in maths, and so forth), but only as exemplification. There was no specific requirement for children to use ICT extensively across the curriculum – indeed, there could not be, as most schools simply did not have sufficient hardware to make this a possibility. The Dearing revision of the National Curriculum in 1995 established IT as a separate subject in its own right, and also included reference in the rubric for each subject (apart from PE) to the effect that IT should be used where appropriate, but gave no indication of what might constitute appropriateness.

The 2000 revision of the National Curriculum included the following statement under General Teaching Requirements.

1. *Pupils should be given opportunities to apply and develop their ICT capability through the use of ICT tools to support their learning in all subjects (with the exception of physical education at Key Stages 1 and 2).*
2. *Pupils should be given opportunities to support their work by being taught to:*
    a. *find things out from a variety of sources, selecting and synthesising the information to meet their needs and developing an ability to question its accuracy, bias and plausibility;*
    b. *develop their ideas using ICT tools to amend and refine their work and enhance its quality and accuracy;*
    c. *exchange and share information, both directly and through electronic media;*
    d. *review, modify and evaluate their work, reflecting critically on its quality, as it progresses.*

A footnote accompanies the first of these statements:

At Key Stage 1, there are no statutory requirements to teach the use of ICT in the Programmes of Study for the non-core foundation subjects. Teachers should use their judgement to decide where it is appropriate to teach the use of ICT across these subjects at Key Stage 1. At other key stages, there are statutory requirements to use ICT in all subjects, except physical education.[43]

How is ICT described in the National Curriculum Programme of Study?

Designing or updating the National Curriculum Programme of Study for ICT is a precarious business, as the subject moves on so rapidly that any definition will seem quaint long before the next review is due. Its designers have gone to some lengths to make it as non-content-specific as possible, without making statements so vague that they are devoid of meaning.

It is perhaps worth reproducing here what the Programme of Study says. Greater detail, examples and links to other subjects, can be found via DfES/QCA.[43]

During Key Stage 1 pupils explore ICT and learn to use it confidently and with purpose to achieve specific outcomes. They start to use ICT to develop their ideas and record their creative work. They become familiar with hardware and software.

***During Key Stage 2** pupils use a wider range of ICT tools and information sources to support their work in other subjects. They develop their research skills and decide what information is appropriate for their work. They begin to question the plausibility and quality of information. They learn how to amend their work and present it in a way that suits its audience.*

These statements are quite important, and quite a lot of current practice, it seems, has not paid them sufficient attention but has tended to concentrate more on teaching children how to use the features of certain programs, without sufficiently considering what they are learning them for.

The Programme of Study identifies four strands under Knowledge, Skills and Understanding:

- *Finding things out.*
- *Developing ideas and making things happen.*
- *Exchanging and sharing information.*
- *Reviewing, modifying and evaluating work as it progresses.*

Additionally, it considers breadth of study.

Note that none of these strands is actually directly about learning about computers, or training to use specific pieces of software. Particularly note also, in the details that follow, how little of the content is conceptualised as an end in itself, and how much may equally be considered in a general, non-computer-centred context, as general good practice and the development of children's thinking skills, study skills and metacognitive awareness. Teaching ICT skills but not providing opportunity to apply them is like giving someone driving lessons but not providing a car.

Finding things out

At Key Stage 1, pupils should be taught how to:

- *gather information from a variety of sources;*
- *enter and store information in a variety of forms;*
- *retrieve information that has been stored.*

At Key Stage 2, pupils should be taught:

- *to talk about what information they need and how they can find and use it;*
- *how to prepare information for development using ICT, including selecting suitable sources, finding information, classifying it and checking it for accuracy;*
- *to interpret information, to check it is relevant and reasonable and to think about what might happen if there were any errors or omissions.*

Developing ideas and making things happen

At Key Stage 1, pupils should be taught:

- *to use text, tables, images and sound to develop their ideas;*
- *how to select from and add to information they have retrieved for particular purposes;*
- *how to plan and give instructions to make things happen;*
- *to try things out and explore what happens in real and imaginary situations.*

At Key Stage 2, pupils should be taught:

- *how to develop and refine ideas by bringing together, organising and reorganising text, tables, images and sound as appropriate;*
- *how to create, test, improve and refine sequences of instructions to make things happen and to monitor events and respond to them;*
- *to use simulations and explore models in order to answer 'What if...?' questions, to investigate and evaluate the effect of changing values and to identify patterns and relationships.*

Exchanging and sharing information

At Key Stage 1, pupils should be taught:

- *how to share their ideas by presenting information in a variety of forms;*
- *to present their completed work effectively.*

At Key Stage 2, pupils should be taught:

- *how to share and exchange information in a variety of forms, including e-mail;*
- *to be sensitive to the needs of the audience and to think carefully about the content and quality when communicating information.*

Reviewing, modifying and evaluating work as it progresses

At Key Stage 1, pupils should be taught to:

- *review what they have done to help them develop their ideas;*
- *describe the effects of their actions;*
- *talk about what they might change in future work.*

At Key Stage 2, pupils should be taught to:

- *review what they and others have done to help them develop their ideas;*
- *describe and talk about the effectiveness of their work with ICT, comparing it with other methods and considering the effect it has on others;*
- *talk about how they could improve future work.*

Breadth of study

During Key Stage I, pupils should be taught the Knowledge, Skills and Understanding through:

- *working with a range of information to investigate the different ways in which it can be presented;*
- *exploring a variety of ICT tools;*
- *talking about the uses of ICT inside and outside school.*

During Key Stage 2, pupils should be taught the Knowledge, Skills and Understanding through:

- *working with a range of information to consider its characteristics and purposes;*
- *working with others to explore a variety of information sources and ICT tools;*
- *investigating and comparing the uses of ICT inside and outside school.*

Skills and techniques

Objectives and intended outcomes for ICT lessons are often expressed in terms that are supposed to characterise the development of ICT skills, though in many cases what is actually being pursued is not strictly a skill at all, but a piece of relatively loca-lised knowledge about how things are currently done in a particular piece of software which may transfer to other pieces of software. A useful distinction can be drawn between a *skill* and a *technique: a skill is something you can get better at.* Making text bold in a word processor is a technique, not a skill – you either know which icon to click on or you do not, and if you do not know it, you can be shown it in a matter of seconds. Knowing how to change a font is not a skill, but developing judgement about when and where to use different fonts, sizes or weights to create a desired effect is a skill, and can be developed to a very sophisticated level.

Reflection

Examine the content of the Programme of Study for a particular key stage, and decide how you might apply the distinction given above between skills and techniques.

What is ICT for?

Twenty years ago, when computers first started to appear in primary schools, there were quite a few teachers who simply could not see the point of them or how their use could possibly impinge on good primary practice – or, indeed, who saw the use of computers as a direct challenge to good practice. Though some teachers still have some reservations about the value of ICT, nobody can now deny that computer technology has become an integral part of our everyday lives, and relatively few people would now consider that computers have no place in the primary curriculum, though their reasons for thinking that might vary.

It will probably come as no surprise to discover that objections to the widespread use of ICT are more likely to be voiced by Early Years practitioners, who may be anxious about a range of issues including the possible detrimental effect of computers on active physical play, or the (largely imagined) tendency of computers to promote social isolation. Perhaps the most influential voice against the use of ICT in an Early Years context has been the Alliance for Childhood's *Fool's Gold* report, published in the USA in 2000.[2] This report, which was supported by some eminent and well-respected educational thinkers, called for a moratorium on the use of computers by children in the Early Years.

Reflection

Read the Executive Summary of the Fool's Gold report. What parts of it, if any, do you agree with? How will that affect your practice?

An ongoing online survey by Twining[86] examines attitudes towards computer use. Respondents are asked to complete a quick questionnaire with respect to the age-group with which they are most familiar. At the time of writing, the question 'Should ICT be an essential component of education?' is answered positively as follows:

Foundation Stage	85%
Key Stage 1	88%
Key Stage 2	92%
Key Stage 3/4	96%

In answer to the question 'Why use ICT in education?' respondents can select from a set of 19 different rationales the three they consider to be the most important for their given age-phase. At the time of writing, the following three rationales are among the top four choices for all three primary phases.

● *In order to extend and enrich learning across the curriculum.*

● *In order to provide access to the curriculum for those who might otherwise be excluded from it.*

● *In order to prepare pupils/students for living in a society that is permeated with technology.*

The other reason that comes within the first four choices for each phase is different, however. For the Foundation Stage it is:

● *In order to motivate learners.*

For Key Stage 1:

● *In order to learn IT skills.*

For Key Stage 2:

- *Because ICT is transforming the nature of knowledge, and thus is a necessary part of learning.*

It is interesting to note that these differences reflect shifts in emphasis between phases. The Early Learning Goals stress familiarisation and motivation; the Key Stage I Programme of Study refers to becoming familiar with hardware and software; the Key Stage 2 Programme of Study considers ICT more in the light of its usefulness across the curriculum.

The Key Stage 3/4 preferences are the same as those for Key Stage 2, though in slightly different proportions.

Rationales chosen by virtually nobody include:

- *In order to increase productivity in education.*
- *In order to reduce the cost of education.*
- *In order to make education more efficient.*
- *As a substitute for teachers.*
- *In order to reward learners.*
- *In order to support and stimulate the computer industry.*

To examine the current state of the survey, or to complete the questionnaire see Twining (2003b).[86] An interim report can be found at Twining (2003a).[85]

Reflection

Have you seen classroom computers used as a reward? ('I've finished my work, Miss – can I play on the computer?')

Or have you done this yourself? Is this ever justifiable?

The ICT Scheme of Work

You will almost certainly be given responsibility for overseeing the ICT Scheme of Work. In many schools the process of teaching ICT has been relatively patchy and haphazard, and the arrival of the QCA Scheme of Work for ICT (QCA, 1998)[72] provided structure and coherence, enabling individual teachers to identify specifically what areas of ICT they were expected to deliver. Though the Scheme is non-statutory, there is a very good chance that your school is making substantial use of it. Think of it as a starting point, but do not allow anyone to think that simply following the Scheme slavishly to the letter is an adequate way of teaching ICT.

As part of its materials for supporting the ICT audit, Worcestershire LEA have produced a Benchmarking Matrix through which schools can grade the current state of their ICT development, with levels defined as Initial, Developmental, Established, or Advanced. It refers to use of the QCA Scheme of Work in these terms:

- *Initial: Teachers are using some elements of the QCA Scheme of Work to plan ICT activities to match their key stage.*
- *Developmental: Teachers are using the QCA Scheme of Work to ensure coverage of the National Curriculum Programmes of Study.*
- *Established: Teachers are adapting some of the QCA Scheme of Work units to respond to pupil need and context.*
- *Advanced: Teachers create or re-design modules of work to extend and/or enrich the level of challenge to best meet the needs of individual pupils.*[93]

Like anything else, an off-the-peg unit of work is only the starting point, as long as you have sufficient confidence in your grasp of the ICT content, and sufficient imagination, enterprise and energy to adapt that unit to meet your own specific circumstances. It may well be that at least some of your colleagues cannot always muster all of those attributes simultaneously. As long as *you* feel you have the energy and imagination, let it be known that you are available for consultation when colleagues are starting to plan how to tackle the designated units, but try not to make your contribution over-technical. Try to feed their imaginations with suggestions about resources, software, websites you know about, but don't take ownership of the unit away from them.

If you do decide, collectively, to design your own scheme of work, make sure that it shows the following:

- *the balance between knowledge, skills and understanding;*
- *how content may best be sequenced to ensure continuity and progression;*
- *what you would expect most pupils to know, understand and be able to do on completion of a unit of work;*
- *links to the wider curriculum;*
- *what resources are required.*

An ICT scheme of work should:
- *provide long- and medium-term plans that show how and when pupils will acquire the knowledge, skills and understanding detailed in the Programme of Study and how the breadth of study will be covered;*
- *provide a secure basis from which teachers can plan lessons to meet the needs of all pupils in a class;*
- *detail the teaching and learning objectives of each unit of work;*
- *identify key ideas so that concepts are built up in an organised, systematic and rigorous way;*
- *identify what pupils are expected to learn, both within a unit and by the end of it, and how their learning may be assessed;*
- *provide opportunities to develop literacy, numeracy, thinking skills and key skills, where appropriate;*
- *have links with other subjects and curriculum areas;*

- *indicate the amount of time needed to teach each unit;*
- *encourage good practice in teaching;*
- *allow for some flexibility when used;*
- *identify key resources and how they might be used with pupils.*

(BECTa)[23]

However your colleagues plan for the implementation of the Scheme of Work, you will need to monitor the process, and offer advice when it is sought – try not to do it for them. You will need to be satisfied that the Programmes of Study have been adequately covered, and be able to give a convincing account of how it all works when OFSTED come to call.

Though ICT has often been identified in inspections as an area of relative weakness, in recent years OFSTED[67] have reported a considerable improvement in the teaching of ICT as a subject. This has been attributed in part to the widespread adoption of the QCA Scheme of Work.

QCA guidance for the amount of time to be spent on generic ICT teaching,[74] which is based on the assumption that children will also have significant opportunities to develop their ICT capability in other subjects, suggests:

- for Key Stage 1, 50 minutes per week, or 30 hours per year;
- for Key Stage 2, 55 minutes per week, or 33 hours per year.

These equate to approximately 4 per cent of the whole timetable.

ICT across the curriculum

Progress in the use of ICT to support and enhance teaching across the curriculum has been relatively slow. One of the difficulties ICT has encountered has been that its potential for use in other subjects has not been sufficiently identified or highlighted by those responsible for the subjects. The National Literacy Strategy (NLS), for example, made a handful of references to word processors as transcription devices, and briefly mentioned spellcheckers, but made no further reference to ICT. Many teachers established the pattern for their Literacy Hours without any reference to the use of ICT at all. An increase in the amount of equipment available, and the advent of the interactive whiteboard and data projector, have significantly altered what it is possible to do, and there is now a concerted effort to shift teachers' perceptions of how ICT might be used to meet existing literacy objectives. Perhaps what is required is a revision of the NLS itself, to take account of the possibilities of new literacies, including the use of digital video (see Chapter 10).

Early pronouncements on the use of ICT in the Literacy Hour were keen to remind teachers that the objectives of the lesson were to be expressed in terms of literacy, not ICT. The assumption was that children would employ ICT skills that they had previously learned elsewhere (presumably in a generic ICT lesson), and that valuable literacy learning time would not be taken up in teaching children to use ICT. That approach has shifted somewhat, and there is now an acknowledgement that children using ICT during the Literacy Hour will almost inevitably also be learning something about ICT.

Learning theory and models of computer use – tutor, tutee and tool

There are various frameworks for thinking about how computers might be used to support learning (see Twining[84]). One model, which was originally proposed by Taylor (1980)[80] suggests three different modes of computer use, which Taylor called tutor, tutee and tool. These modes have their antecedents in different theories of learning.

Tutor

> The computer presents some subject material, the student responds, the computer evaluates the response, and, from the results of the evaluation, determines what to present next.
>
> (Taylor, 1980, page 3)[80]

This mode has its origins in behaviourism, and particularly in the ideas of B.F. Skinner. Behaviourism was the predominant school of thought in learning theory in the middle decades of the twentieth century, though few people would now accept it as an adequate model to account for all learning. Skinner's theory of operant conditioning was based on the positive reinforcement of desirable behaviour, and he argued for the breaking down of learning processes into small steps, with positive reinforcement after each step. He proposed a teaching machine:

> The important features of the device are these: reinforcement for the right answer is immediate. The mere manipulation of the device will probably be reinforcing enough to keep the average student at work for a suitable period each day, provided traces of earlier aversive control can be wiped out. A teacher may supervise an entire class at work on such devices at the same time, yet each child may progress at his own rate, completing as many problems as possible within the class period. If forced to be away from school, he may return where he left off... The device makes it possible to present carefully designed material in which one problem can depend upon the answer to the preceding and where, therefore, the most progress to an eventually complex repertoire can be made.
>
> (Skinner, 1968)[77]

Teaching machines of this sort had a brief heyday in the 1960s. Their natural successors, at a more sophisticated level, are computer-based Integrated Learning Systems (ILS), which some schools have invested in. The claimed advantages of an ILS are very similar to the points that Skinner made:

- that reinforcement or praise for correct responses is immediate;
- that individual pupils can work at their own pace;
- that the computer is infinitely patient, and does not damage the pupil's self-esteem, e.g. through expressions of exasperation;

- that assessments of pupils' responses are stored electronically, and can be used to make judgements about individuals' progress within the subject being taught.

Against this, however, a number of objections might be raised, including:

- that it reduces the idea of learning within a subject area to responses to a series of problems on a screen;
- that the computer can only know that a pupil has given an incorrect response – it has no information about why that response was incorrect so it cannot efficiently address and correct a misconception;
- that there is relatively little evidence that 'skills' learned in this sort of context transfer to any other context.

Manufacturers of ILS tend to make large claims for the amount of progress children make while using them. Independent evaluations have tended to be much more cautious, and suggest that there may be some advantage in using an ILS to consolidate other learning, and that in fact the greatest progress is made when an adult mediates the process rather than when the child works through the program alone. For further information, see Underwood and Brown (1997),[87] Wood (1998).[91]

A lot of subject-specific software is loosely based on the notion that the role of the computer is to be a teacher. Probably most of the 'education' software designed for the home market falls into this category, where children undertake endless drill-and-practice exercises while cute cartoon characters tell them how wonderful they are every time they give a correct response.

Tutee

One of the principal objections to behaviourism is that it views learning as little more than the passive reception of knowledge, of memorising facts. Constructivism, on the other hand, views learning as the construction of knowledge within the head of the individual learner, of integrating new experiences and information with existing concepts. Teaching is therefore thought of as the process that supports the construction and reconstruction of new knowledge rather than the process of communicating knowledge. Probably the best-known constructivist thinker was Piaget. Seymour Papert, who worked with Piaget, is the inventor of LOGO, the computer application (or, strictly speaking, the computer language) that best illustrates the computer in the role of tutee. In teaching the computer a series of procedures to construct an object, users are engaged in the process of formulating and testing hypotheses. Papert referred to computers as *objects to think with* (Papert, 1980).[70]

Taylor identifies three advantages of using the computer in this way:

- *You will learn what you are trying to teach the computer, because you can't teach something you don't know about yourself.*
- *As the computer can only operate within narrow confines this will force you to think about how to teach the computer and in so doing will force you to think about how your own thinking works.*

● *Teachers can save time and money by using computers as tutees because they don't have to locate and pay for tutor or tool software.*

The basic premise underpinning the tutee mode of computer use is that:

> ... *in teaching the computer, the child learns more deeply and learns more about the process of learning than he or she does from being tutored by software written by others.*
>
> (Taylor, 1980, page 9)[80]

Use of LOGO in primary schools in the UK has been somewhat sporadic, though there are several countries where it forms a major part of the ICT curriculum. On the other hand, there is hardly a primary school in the country that does not make use of *Roamer*, or a similar floor robot, in more or less exactly the same role.

Tool

Much of the time that computers are being used effectively in a cross-curricular context, they are being used as tools – word-processors, databases, spreadsheets, graphics programs and so forth. Taylor, writing more than two decades ago, was somewhat dismissive of the learning benefits to be gained from using the computer in this way:

> *Use of the computer in tool mode may teach the user something during use, but any such teaching is most likely accidental and not the result of a design to teach.*
>
> (Taylor, 1980, page 8)[80]

Much current thinking about how children learn is based on the ideas of Vygotsky. Social constructivist theory has much in common with Piaget, but does not accept the Piagetian model of the child-as-lone-scientist. Rather, it emphasises the importance of the social context for cognitive development. The best-known concept from Vygotsky's work is probably the zone of proximal development (ZPD) – what children can do aided today, they can do unaided tomorrow. Learning is essentially social, and children learn best when working collaboratively in groups, but adults can scaffold children's experiences to keep them operating within their ZPD. School learning should emphasise meaningful, authentic, 'real-world' contexts. This leads to a mode of operation for ICT that stresses the middle C – communication – and makes the use of the computer as a tool the most powerfully educative of the three modes. Most importantly, the computer can mediate the learning experience, or can be the agent through which learners can reach a shared understanding of what they are learning. The computer-as-tool can assist in the process of coming-to-know.

Reflection

Consider the software that you would expect to use in your classroom. In which of the three modes are children most likely to be operating when they use it? What are the implications of this?

Summary

There has been a certain amount of confusion between ICT as a subject and ICT as a tool to enhance teaching and learning across the curriculum. OFSTED report that the teaching of the subject, though it has been weak, is now improving substantially. In overseeing the delivery of the Programme of Study through your Scheme of Work, you should ensure that skills are developed and not merely techniques, and that children have the opportunity to make use of those skills in other subjects. Though there is some agreement among teachers about what ICT is for, more needs to be done to make effective use of ICT to enhance or transform learning and teaching across the curriculum.

7 EQUIPMENT, LOCATIONS AND PEDAGOGY

(→) According to the National Standards for Subject Leadership, you should:

- establish staff and resource needs and advise the headteacher and senior managers of likely priorities for expenditure, and allocate available resources with maximum efficiency to meet the objectives of the school and subject plans and achieve value for money;
- ensure the effective and efficient management and organisation of learning resources, including information and communications technology;
- maintain existing resources and explore opportunities to develop or incorporate new resources from a wide range of sources inside and outside the school;
- use accommodation to create an effective and stimulating environment for the teaching and learning of the subject;
- ensure that there is a safe working and learning environment in which risks are properly assessed.

Your responsibility is for ICT, and of course ICT means more than just computers, though the sense in which it also encompasses television, tape recorders and a range of other things that plug in seems to be sliding out of general usage. You would probably not expect it to be part of your job to set the school video. ICT definitely still includes printers, scanners, equipment for datalogging and control (including programmable devices like *Roamer* or *Pixie*), calculators, digital cameras and digital video, and, particularly in the Foundation Stage, all sorts of electronic toys. Some schools have sets of small palmtop machines, and over the next few years you can expect to see an increase in the use of other handheld devices to support the primary curriculum.

This book cannot tell you how to deploy the resources you have at your disposal as decisions will be heavily coloured by specific local circumstances. It can, however, alert you to some of the issues you should consider if you are to put the equipment you have to the best possible use.

In some cases, decisions will already have been taken at a higher level with which you will need to comply – or, if you see a pressing need to alter things, you will need to construct a compelling case to do so. One such decision might involve the designation of a classroom or other teaching space as a computer room or suite. For the sake of simplicity, this chapter will assume that your computer suite is a single enclosed room rather than a cluster of machines in an open activity area or anything else, and that it contains desktop machines rather than laptops. This may not accord with reality as you find it, but to cater for all the various possibilities equally would render this chapter unreadable.

A decade ago, computer rooms were a rarity in primary schools, though they have long been standard in secondary schools. Reasons for their ubiquity in the secondary context include:

● the teaching of computer studies as a subject;

● the fact that secondary school timetables are organised around the movement of pupils from room to room;

● the relative ease of networking a computer room by comparison with a whole building;

● the simple fact that secondary schools have more computers, and a better computer-to-pupil ratio than primary schools;

● the security of expensive equipment is easier to maintain if they are kept in one room with a suitable alarm system;

● the pedagogy is based on the model of one person per machine.

Of course, it is now quite usual for secondary schools to have a number of computer rooms.

Primary school pedagogy for ICT, on the other hand, has developed from:

● a relative lack of equipment;

● a model of use where children characteristically worked in twos and threes at a machine;

● the absence of identifiable spare rooms in which a computer suite could be housed;

● the expectation that most of the activity of a class would be contained within one room or work area.

Also, until e-mail and the internet became realistic and worthwhile activities in a primary context, there was relatively little reason to network machines at all, so there was no advantage to be gained in terms of saving on the cost of cabling by keeping machines together in one place.

A decade ago, the computers most commonly found in primary classrooms (though this varied from local authority to local authority) were those produced by Acorn, the manufacturer of the BBC 'B'. In recent years Acorn as a firm has disappeared, and although Acorn-style computers are still manufactured it is very unlikely that any school or LEA will invest heavily in them. In most places the dominant computer is the PC, usually running a version of Microsoft Windows as its operating system, though there are some areas of the country in which Apple computers are widely used and, particularly as the use of digital video is expanding rapidly as an exciting area of ICT use, there are signs that the Apple share of the market might be increasing.

The demise of Acorn is perhaps a cause of some regret. Many classic pieces of primary educational software were designed originally on Acorn machines, and some may be thought to have lost something in translation to PC versions. When businesses used PCs and schools used Acorns, it was easier for primary schools to keep hold of the agenda for educational ICT, and not be sidetracked into ICT activities that were only marginally appropriate to the primary curriculum because they happened to be what PCs were good at and widely used for.

In 1997 the Stevenson Report[78] noted with some alarm that a large proportion of school computers were fairly old, and recommended that when one counted how many computers a school had one should not count anything over five years old. A number of factors came together to influence the way in which primary hardware provision changed as the millennium changed. The establishment of the National Grid for Learning,[64] and vastly increased government spending on hardware for schools has coincided with a huge expansion in the range and scope of the internet, so that it has become a plausible resource for general use in the primary school. For several years it had been fairly common for OFSTED school reports to identify ICT as an area of relative weakness. The rapid growth in home computer ownership has meant that the clear majority of children have access to a machine outside school, and in many cases spend far longer on ICT activities at home than they do at school.

Given the particular combination of circumstances, it is perhaps not surprising that so many schools suddenly managed to find the space to dedicate a room or area as a computer room or suite. The space identified might once have been the library or the music practice room. For a while, it seemed that many schools gathered up the computers that were dispersed throughout their classes, and put them together in one place, or else they jettisoned the ageing machines in the classrooms, but put all the new replacements in the computer room. Either way, we have been through a period in which many schools have had a brand new computer room, but no computers available in the classroom (or sometimes a residual old Acorn machine waiting to be pensioned off).

Reflection

If you have a computer room or suite, identify five ways in which it is advantageous, and five ways in which it is not a good idea.

If you do not have a computer room or suite, identify five significant advantages that could be gained by establishing one, and five principal objections to doing so.

Setting up a computer room

If you find yourself in the position where you are being asked to set up a new computer room, these are some points to consider.

- The overall responsibility for this task rests with the head teacher and the senior management team. Even if you seem to be given a free hand, make sure you liaise carefully with them and keep them actively engaged in the process.

- This is a whole-school decision. Everyone has ownership of the room, and you really want all potential users to feel comfortable using it and not to feel that they are trespassing on someone else's territory.

- There are different responsibilities relating to the upkeep and development of the room. Some are general, e.g. there is an expectation that every class will leave the room substantially as they found it, but there are also some more specific tasks, like having overall responsibility for display within the room. If possible, try to agree that these responsibilities should be shared out among colleagues – cast your net as wide as possible, but do not lumber anyone with a chore they do not want.

- If you are starting from scratch and you have sufficient space to allow you some choice in the matter, think carefully about exactly how you wish to deploy the equipment in the room. Do not assume that placing the machines around the walls or in serried ranks are the only layout options. There are several other possibilities (like placing machines in clusters), each with its advantages and drawbacks. Space precludes detailed discussion here, but see, for example the information provided by BECTa.[10]

- You will probably wish to establish a means of whole-class demonstration, and increasingly this means you will have a data projector and perhaps an interactive whiteboard. Obviously, you must arrange your computer room in such a way that every child can see the screen, board or projected image. You can install systems that allow you to place the image from one computer onto the screens of all the others. Though this is perhaps better than nothing, it is not really a suitable way to conduct a demonstration – it is much better to be able to make eye contact with everyone, and of course absolutely essential to be able to do so if you are intending to teach interactively and engage the class in discussion or expect children to contribute to demonstrations, for example by moving objects on the whiteboard.

- If you have a data projector, it is better to have this ceiling-mounted, as:

  - it will not get damaged by being knocked over;
  - the bulb is likely to last longer if the projector cannot be moved – and replacement bulbs are amazingly expensive;
  - the extent to which you will be working in your own shadow is reduced;
  - the angle of projection will reduce the possibility of the bright light adversely affecting your eyesight;
  - properly secured, it is probably safer from casual theft than a portable device – though it will never be completely safe from a really determined thief.

- A common failing of primary school computer rooms is to place computers close together, making it impossible for two or more children to work at a single machine at the same time. Try to space machines so that children can sit comfortably at them – see the health and safety notes in Chapter 3.

- Ensure that heights of chairs, benches and monitors are appropriate for the users. As there is a huge difference in size between a Nursery or Reception pupil and a Year 6 pupil, if both are expected to use the same suite you will need to ensure that chair heights, at least, are adjustable.[10] Some larger or better off primary schools now have more than one dedicated computer room.

- As we saw in Chapter 6, the one-per-machine model is often inappropriate. In fact, there is sometimes a case to be made for *reducing* the number of computers in a room – if, for example, you have 20 computers and 25 children in a class, children will assume they are supposed to have one each but there are not enough to go around, whereas if you had only 15 machines with more space between them, they are more likely to accept that they will be working in pairs. You could probably find other worthwhile locations for the surplus machines elsewhere in the school.

- There are, of course, occasions when you *do* want children to work one-per-machine, particularly if your school has invested in an Integrated Learning System (ILS).

- The probability at the moment is that the machines in the computer room are physically connected to a network. For your own peace of mind, it is better if the network server is a separate machine, located apart from the rest of the machines in the suite. Servers are sometimes placed in storage cupboards, but this can lead to frustration when the network goes down and you (or whoever manages it) have to work in discomfort to put things right.

Display

For some reason, displays on the walls of computer rooms seem to change less often than displays in other parts of the school. One reason for this is that, inevitably, some of what is being displayed will be lists of instructions relating to the use of the room or prompt sheets to support basic functions like printing or particular software applications, all of which need to remain on a more or less permanent basis. As suggested above, unless you are particularly keen on display, this is one function you may be able to delegate to a colleague. Post the instructions prominently, probably in several parts of the room, including reminders to children to save their work regularly. If you have high ceilings, make use of higher wall space to display, for example, children's graphic designs – change these on a regular basis. By all means be more imaginative by hanging mobiles or converting parts of the room into different 'environments', but particularly bear in mind health and safety considerations, including the need to have adequate ventilation. Computer rooms can become unpleasantly warm.

Computers are stolen. Even more precious to thieves, currently, are data projectors. It has been the custom in many secondary schools to leave computer rooms locked when they are not in use. The school will need to decide what policy to adopt with regard to your computer room. You will need to make sure the room is basically secure (and preferably has an alarm system) and that the door is locked before the premises are vacated at night. You will probably want to leave the room accessible for individual users during times when it is not booked out to a class. Most primary schools now have locked outside doors, and it is harder for a stranger to gain access while the school is in session. The grey areas are outside the teaching day, when you might have a breakfast club, homework club or after-school computer club. There are no hard and fast rules, but be security conscious.

Reflection

How secure is your computer equipment?

How do you balance the need for good security with the need for easy access by children, and the need to make your computer room an attractive place?

A thorough discussion of issues to do with setting up a computer room is provided by BECTa.[10] You should not attempt to set up a computer room without reading this document carefully. It is probable that your LEA will also have some advice to offer, no doubt including factual information about local suppliers of hardware, furniture, etc. It is worth paying a visit to some other local schools to see how they have set up their rooms. Though this should not be your particular responsibility, it is of course necessary to cost the whole exercise carefully, bearing in mind that the hardware is not necessarily the most expensive factor and on-costs can be very substantial.

Conducting an audit of resources

The auditing of resources will form part of the overall ICT audit as a precursor to the ICT development plan (see Chapter 4). If your predecessor as ICT co-ordinator has done the job efficiently, there should be a written record or inventory of all the hardware, software and peripheral equipment held by the school, including details of the date of purchase, serial numbers, the location of the equipment, warranty details and any service record that might be relevant. If this has been done meticulously, all well and good, but you should still conduct your own audit, and as far as possible (depending perhaps on the size of your school), you should visit all the equipment and visualise it for yourself. It is a good idea, where feasible, to conduct this audit at the same time as the audit of staff skills etc., in order to help you to match equipment to needs and identify areas and priorities for future development.

If there is no such inventory of hardware, you will need to establish one. If possible, do not attempt to do this alone. If you can cajole people into it (and the head teacher into providing sufficient time to do it), work with a teacher colleague and at least one classroom assistant, so that the system you establish is well understood by others and can continue in your absence. There should be no difficulty over establishing the purchase date of most current hardware, and for anything clearly over five years old the actual date of purchase is largely irrelevant. Keep the equipment inventory in paper form, and also on a database or spreadsheet file which can be updated periodically.

Managed services

Some schools operate within a managed service, whereby an outside agency undertakes to provide, maintain and replace machines as required, in return for a fixed fee. There are various ways in which this can operate, with varying degrees of commitment by either party. Managed services may often appear expensive, but they need not be any more expensive than going it alone. In making calculations about the cost of ICT resources, schools often underestimate the on-costs.

There are some advantages to be had from this sort of arrangement. It makes your life much easier knowing that machines in need of repair will be replaced immediately, and that the rolling replacement of ageing machines is being managed. Because that side of things is taken care of, you have more time to think about pedagogic issues.

On the other hand, there will inevitably be some loss of autonomy. You may have little say in precisely what computers are supplied; if the managed service is also responsible for the maintenance of your network, there may for example be some conditions imposed on you which do not mesh easily with your pedagogic priorities. Also, signing up to a managed system is usually a long-term commitment, and you may find you have insufficient flexibility if your priorities change substantially as the technology develops (as they no doubt will).

Connecting to the internet

By 2006, all schools should have a broadband connection – see the information provided by BECTa.[24] It is quite likely that your LEA has a policy in relation to connecting schools, and you would be well advised to get involved with it, not least because it should provide a level of technical support you are unlikely to be able to supply for yourself. On the whole, however well-intentioned and well-informed it might be, you should probably decline the offer from the parent or governor who works in the industry and can provide you with a different supplier. Broadband connection makes internet access much faster than any other type of connection, and it means that you can leave your connection permanently switched on. A broadband connection should easily cope with all your school computers accessing the internet simultaneously. It will also enable, for example, the use of real-time video material. In a decade's time, anything slower than broadband will look as primitive as black and white television.

The firewall

If you do not currently have broadband, the probability is that you have an ISDN line, or possibly ADSL (see the BECTa ICT Advice Sheet).[20] In any event, it is now absolutely essential to the security of your system that you have a firewall in place. According to BECTa, this can help to:

- *prevent malicious users on the internet from accessing data or services on a private network;*

- *defend the private network against 'attack';*

- *control access from the internet to ensure that only certain services on the private network ... are available to external users;*

- *hide the private network from the internet;*

- *control access between two parts of a private network (for example to prevent classroom users from having access to office/administrative facilities);*

- *allow some forms of internet access and deny others (for instance, to allow web browsing but deny the use of streaming audio or internet relay chat).*

In addition, although this is not their primary function, firewalls can:

- *protect your network from attempts to exploit well-known insecurities in web browsers and other client software (by denying access to that software);*

- *provide some measure of protection against certain forms of computer virus such as 'worms'and 'trojans'...; although this is the role of a dedicated virus checker, it may run on the same hardware as the firewall.*

A BECTa Technical Paper on firewalls[17] explains this in much greater detail.

Viruses

You should also install a good virus checker on all school computers, whether or not they are on the network. Most viruses are spread by e-mail (and particularly through 'infected' attachments), and some can do significant damage to the operation of your system, though it is possible to overstate this. Virus protection software will guard your system against infection, from whatever source. It may well be the case that your LEA has obtained a licence for virus protection software which they will make available to you either free or else at a discount. On the whole, you should not then need to be over-anxious about the risk of infection from pupils bringing in floppy disks or CD-ROMs from home. Some schools adopt a policy of not allowing anything from outside the school to be placed on the school system. Though this might be sound policy in terms of avoiding clogging your system with non-educational software, the risk of infection is relatively slight as long as your virus protection software is up to date. Preventing pupils from using files of work they have prepared at home is almost certainly educationally counter-productive – though you would be wise to insist that children seek permission before using their own disks, and that they always do so under supervision. Some useful advice about viruses can be found at the Devon LEA website.[31]

As ICT co-ordinator you will almost certainly receive regular communications from staff or others regarding e-mail warnings about viruses. Almost always, these are hoaxes, and although most are harmless, a few advise users to delete files from their machines which could possibly be essential to the operation of the machine. You should never pass the warning on to anyone else without checking first to see if it is genuine. A good place to check first is the Symantec site.[79]

Printers

You need to have a policy regarding the use of printers. It is well-established that a printer is an essential part of any educational ICT facility. Children derive great satisfaction from seeing their work printed out, and it is often necessary to keep printouts for purposes of assessment and evaluation. However, printing can be a very expensive option, particularly if every computer is equipped with a colour inkjet printer. The printers themselves are very inexpensive, but the cost of replacement cartridges is very high, and it will erode your overall ICT budget disproportionately unless you keep their use in check.

- Firstly, consider whether each computer needs its own printer at all. Where machines are networked, it is relatively simple to direct all printing to one printer, in which case it makes sense to invest in a good quality laser printer to handle the work. The printer may cost more, but the unit cost per page is much lower than for an inkjet printer and the quality of the printout is much higher. On the other hand, children need the reassurance that their work is actually printing out, and if the printer is in a remote location they may not see it happen. There is a well-known tendency for some children to click on 'print' many times, in order to help it on its way!

- Second, consider whether every printer needs to have colour. Colour inkjet cartridges are very expensive, and if they contain wells for all three colours they tend to be thrown away when the first colour runs out, which is very wasteful. On the other hand, nobody who has spent time designing, say, a wonderful coloured poster wants to see it printed out in shades of grey. Again, if machines are networked, you will normally have the option of sending printing work to a choice of printers – set your default choices to monochrome, so that users have to make a conscious choice to print in colour. Colour laser printers are now becoming a realistic option.

You may have to square this policy with some colleagues, in which case you should monitor the actual cost of printing and present the figures at a staff meeting.

Teaching in a computer room

If you are taking your whole class to work in the computer room, think about how you let them enter the room. If all machines are identical, and all are in perfect working order, it does not particularly matter who works at which machine. If this is not the case, however, you can be quite certain, particularly with older classes, that some children are well aware of which machines to avoid, and they will make a bee-line for the better, more reliable machines. This tends to be a characteristic of boys who are (or who think of themselves as being) relatively sophisticated computer users. Unless you are careful, the children who have the greatest need of access to school computers will be the ones who find themselves working with the least reliable equipment, which is unlikely to boost their confidence as users of ICT. Have a strategy in place to cope with this – have a means of determining, and varying, the order in which children enter the room; if machines are generally all reliable anyway, perhaps allocate particular children to particular machines and stick with the arrangement.

Children will need to log on to the network. This should be the first thing they do when they are settled at a machine. Train them not to wait to be asked. If your system is well set up, this should be a fairly automatic process for them. They should enter or select their user ID, then enter their password. You must be very strict about applying the rules here — do not let anyone reveal their password to anyone else, and do not write down a list of passwords. It is essential that you have administrator rights on your network system, because there will always be someone who has forgotten their password and you will need to rescue the situation. If you are fortunate enough to have a technician on site, they should also have administrator rights. You will need to decide also who else among the teaching staff and teaching assistants needs to have administrator rights. If nobody apart from you can get into the system, you will forever have people knocking on your classroom door while you are teaching.

If, as is often the case, the lesson starts with a demonstration by you, unless you have a system in place that allows you to lock all the keyboards from your machine, tell the children to turn off the monitors on their computers. If your room has been equipped with health and safety considerations in mind, the chairs will be adjustable and will also swivel. Show children how to vary the height of their seat when they first use the room, but make it clear that sensible conduct in the room, which they have agreed to maintain, includes not treating the chairs as fairground rides.

Conventionally, the demonstration is followed by some hands-on activity by the children. As far as possible, arrange things so that children can be self-maintaining while they work — generally, working in pairs is a good idea. Try to ensure that the children with the most thorough understanding of computers are spaced around the room, and establish it as policy that children are expected to support each other. The alternative to this is that you are likely to spend much of your time rushing around from machine to machine sorting out minor glitches and trivial misconceptions, and all the carefully considered key questions you had prepared will never see the light of day.

As your session in the computer room is timed, always issue warnings to children before it is time to finish the hands-on session. A five-minute warning followed by another one or two minutes before the end is recommended. Remind children that they need to save their work if they will be returning to it at a later stage.

As with the Literacy Hour and the daily mathematics lesson, you should finish your session with a plenary. If you have remembered to issue time warnings, you should not have to battle against children anxiously trying to finish something or save something while the plenary is taking place. Use this as an opportunity for children to show and celebrate what they have done, to discuss the decisions they had to make in the process, to evaluate what they have achieved and to think ahead to what they will do next. At the end of the plenary, remind the children to log out before leaving the room.

Internet safety

This is a large and important area, and you will be expected to be well-informed about all aspects of it, and be able to offer advice to the head teacher and senior management team, to teaching and non-teaching colleagues, to governors and to parents. It is an area that causes considerable anxiety, and your task is to establish and maintain a robust policy without unnecessarily shutting down the huge educational possibilities offered by the internet. Of course you have to exercise caution and vigilance, and subject your policy to a rigorous risk-assessment process; however, a number of schools have allowed themselves to be panicked into setting down policies that are perhaps over-cautious, including banning direct access to the internet altogether.

Fortunately, the issues are quite well documented (though they go well beyond the scope of this book). You should familiarise yourself with the content of the DfES Superhighway Safety site,[38] and draw the attention of parents to the Superhighway Safety site for parents.[39] If you ensure that your policies are broadly in line with the information contained in these sites, you should be able to allay most of the parental anxieties that are voiced in your direction. Another excellent starting point is the Kent Schools Internet Policy site,[53] which gives you a clear and detailed rationale for the use of the internet, as well as a sample Acceptable Use Policy (see below) and sample letters to parents, etc.

- You may well have a 'walled garden' system, or some other means of filtering the sites to which children have access, like *Net Nanny*.[60]

- You should be aware of the NGfL *GridWatch* site.[61]

- You might prefer to provide children with a safe internet search engine, like *Yahooligans!*[94]

- If your children make use of e-mail, or any sort of chat room facility, either at school or at home, they need to be well-informed about the potential hazards, and the rules they should adopt for their own safety. For older children, make use of the NGfL *KidSmart* site,[62] or perhaps the Disney *Cybernetiquette Comix*.[45] You should also be aware of *GridClub*[50] – see Chapter 9.

In practice, if primary children wilfully and surreptitiously deflect their internet activity away from the task you intended, it generally seems to be towards the websites of Manchester United or the latest boy band – but you can never be too careful.

Acceptable Use Policy

If your school does not already have an Acceptable Use Policy (see the information provided by BECTa[22]), make it a priority to establish one immediately. An Acceptable Use Policy is a contract between the school and the children and their parents, guardians or carers. Its purpose is to set down some clear rules and guidelines relating to the use of the internet in school, and also (probably) to offer some guidance about the use of the internet at home. It aims to protect children from exposure to undesirable materials, while at the same time promoting responsible use of the internet in as wide a sense as possible. The policy itself might be quite detailed and long, but for primary age children there should be a clear statement of rules, taking up no more than one side of A4, which should be posted close to any computer on which children have internet access. No child should have access to the internet until they (and/or their parents) have signed the agreement, and any deliberate transgressions of the rules should be dealt with by withdrawal of that access.

As a matter of policy, you should insist that the agreement should be signed, and the rules adhered to, by *all* users of your system, not just the children.

Setting rules for the use of the computer room

It is usually a good idea to discuss and agree the rules of the computer room with children so that they feel some sense of ownership of them. These will of course include general safety rules, the internet safety rules and acceptable use conditions, but you may well wish to establish some other rules relating to the effective use of the room. Express your rules as positives wherever you can – i.e. in terms of what you should do, rather than what you should not do.

Reflection

What would you do if any children wilfully disregarded the rules?

What would you do if any of your colleagues did so?

Whole-class teaching with ICT

Until fairly recently there was very little chance of using a single computer with a whole class. The problem, of course, was with the need for everyone to see the same screen at the same time. Computer monitor sizes are measured diagonally like televisions, and the rule of thumb that has sometimes been used is one inch per pupil, so that, for example, it is just about possible for half a class to read reasonably large text on a 17-inch screen, though it is rarely satisfactory to do so. It is now becoming far more usual for schools to have data projectors, and perhaps interactive whiteboards, by means of which whole class teaching can be achieved. In 2002, 44 per cent of primary schools had at least one interactive whiteboard,[37] though we are still some way away from most schools having these permanently available in every classroom. Opposition to the idea of the interactive whiteboard has come mostly from people who fear it will be used as a way of encouraging teachers to stand at the front of the class and lecture children. In your capacity as ICT co-ordinator you will need to be aware of that possibility, discuss good practice with your colleagues and quietly monitor the situation to see if that is how whiteboards are in fact being used.

It might be argued that though the computer room needs a data projector in order to produce a large image, the need for an interactive whiteboard there is slightly less than it is in an ordinary classroom – as the children have their own computers to work with, the demonstration part of the lesson does not need to be particularly interactive, in the sense of coming out and having a go.

As a matter of policy, as more interactive whiteboards become available, arrange for them to be placed in classes across the age range in your school, and ensure that the training teachers receive is not confined to showing them how to operate the board but includes discussions with existing users (perhaps including teachers from other schools) about how to make the most educationally effective use of them. One small, simple technicality that can be overlooked is that small children (and short teachers!) cannot reach the tops of wall-mounted boards if they are mounted too high. If your interactive whiteboard is wall-mounted and the data projector is ceiling-mounted, you do not need to adjust or calibrate them at the start of every session. For Early Years classes there is something to be said for working with a small portable interactive whiteboard, which can be set on a stand on a table. This makes for a much more intimate usage, particularly if classes or groups are seated on the carpet in front of it.

The point of the interactive whiteboard is that it should facilitate interactive teaching. Whatever subject you use it in, look for opportunities to use it as the matrix upon which you and your children plan, discuss and create something, edit and modify it, store it and revisit it. Also, do not overlook the possibilities of a group of children working collaboratively at an interactive whiteboard.

Group teaching with ICT

It has been usual for classroom computers to be placed on trolleys or benching against the wall. This is unsurprising, as that is where the power points are likely to be, and for health and safety reasons you cannot have wires trailing across thoroughfares in your classroom. One unfortunate consequence of this has been that children have had to work with their backs to the rest of the class, and it is not normally possible to seat more than about three children at a single computer. This is a shame, as there are some very worthwhile things that can be done with an ordinary computer and a larger group. In the Literacy Hour, for example, you could use a computer with a group of six children, or even a double group, if you could all place yourselves suitably around the machine.

Here is one way to do it. Arrange a group of tables so that one side is touching or close to the wall or the benching at the side of the room – it does not really matter which, as long as there is no thoroughfare between the table and the wall. Place the monitor (and if necessary the plinth) on the wall side of the table, facing inwards. Place the keyboard and mouse in the middle of the table. Seat the children and yourself around the other three sides of the table, so that everyone can reach the keyboard and mouse. Suppose your objectives are to add a paragraph after a given story opening – present that opening on a word-processor. Discuss as a group what might happen next, then ask children to work in pairs, or whatever, to crystallise their ideas. When they are ready, decide between you what to type in, and take it in turns to add it to the text on the screen – and so on. There is room on the table for their books and their pencil-cases. As everyone can reach the mouse and keyboard, nobody need monopolise them.

There are several ways in which you might use a computer to work in collaboration with a group, but in practice this very rarely happens.

Reflection

Can you think of three other ways in which you might use a computer to work collaboratively with a group of children?

What would be the advantages of doing so, and what problems would you have to overcome?

Children working in twos and threes

Primary ICT pedagogy evolved from not having very many computers, and it has been usual to expect children to work in twos and threes, partly to speed up the rate at which everyone will have their turn, but also partly because of an expectation that collaborative work will be educationally enriching. Many claims have been made for the quality of language interaction in this context, though the situation is not always as rosy as it is depicted (Wegerif and Scrimshaw, 1997).[90] Depending on the nature of the task being undertaken, it has been disappointingly uncommon to see children collaborating and reaching a shared understanding of what is to be done. All too often, the child with the mouse is in complete control, and the others are little more than spectators. Taking turns partly alleviates this, but it does not solve the problem. It has been shown that it is possible to teach children to collaborate more effectively, and that the quality of their work improves when this has been done. See, in particular, the various publications at *Thinking Together*.[81] The problem is more acute when the computer is operating as tutor and less so when it is a tool which mediates children's developing ideas. Think carefully about the nature of the task children are being asked to undertake, and what you actually expect them to learn from it. If you are grouping children in twos or threes, think carefully about who you place with whom, and monitor the ways in which they interact. Is one group member dominant? Is anyone being a mere spectator? The danger is that the ones who need the most practice at using the computer are often the ones who get the least. There is no simple solution to this, beyond monitoring and well-timed intervention by you.

Laptop computers and wireless networks

In an ideal world, how many computers would you like in your classroom? When this question usually implied filling up wall space with cumbersome computer trolleys, most classrooms would have found it difficult to accommodate more than two. However, the world has moved on.

If circumstances and funds permit, you might consider establishing a wireless local area network (WLAN) in your school. For this, you need a base station and your computers need to be fitted with wireless cards. This will enable individual computers to communicate with the base station as long as they are in range (possibly about 100 metres depending on a number of factors, including what your school is made of).

Primary schools are beginning to invest in sets of laptop computers, which can communicate with each other and can access the internet by means of the wireless network. Perhaps the most effective way of managing the set is to invest in a trolley that plugs into the mains and charges all the batteries while the computers are being stored.

There are some obvious advantages to be had:

- Laptops can be taken anywhere, do not need to be plugged into anything and occupy relatively little space, so you can take the technology to the learning rather than having to take the learning to the technology. Children can work with the computer at their own table, or take the computer outside to record observations at the bird table or the pond, and so forth.

- This considerably increases the flexibility of your resources – the whole set could be used by one class or the machines could be dispersed among several classes as circumstances dictate. Though this needs to be timetabled, it causes less disruption than moving whole classes backwards and forwards to a computer room, and reduces the need to dovetail ICT work into a particular timeslot.

In practice, there are some issues of which you should be aware:

- Laptop computers are more expensive than desktop machines. This needs to be a consideration when you are thinking of replacing old desktop computers.

- Laptop batteries do not last as long as you might like them to. Children need to be well-drilled to save their work regularly, and you might need to have some provision to make it possible to plug a few machines into the mains to avoid the disappointment of losing work.

- At present wireless networking is not particularly quick, and if a whole class is engaged in an internet-intensive exercise at the same time you will probably notice a loss of speed.

- Many laptop screens have a fairly limited angle of vision; you need to face the screen fairly straight on in order to see it properly. This is an issue if you are expecting three or four children to work collaboratively at one laptop – it is difficult to hold a discussion when your heads are nearly touching.

Some children (and some adults) really struggle to control the pointer on a laptop computer. It is probably worthwhile to buy a set of mice. Simple straightforward mice are very inexpensive; small mice, suitable for use by small hands, are also relatively inexpensive, and take up a very small amount of space for storage.

Summary

In recent years there has been a rapid movement towards the creation of computer rooms in primary schools. Though this is generally a good thing, and it has had a beneficial effect on the teaching of ICT as a subject, there are a number of factors you should take into account when setting up a room and when teaching in it. In particular, you need a clear policy with regard to internet safety. Presentation devices like data projectors and interactive whiteboards have opened up the possibilities for whole-class interactive teaching with ICT across the curriculum; you should also consider ways in which groups and pairs of children can be effectively supported. A rapidly developing alternative to the computer room is a wireless network of laptop computers.

8 TEACHING, ASSESSING AND EVALUATING

(→) According to the National Standards for Subject Leadership, you should:

- ensure teachers are clear about the teaching objectives in lessons, understand the sequence of teaching and learning in the subject and communicate such information to pupils;
- ensure guidance is provided on the choice of appropriate teaching and learning methods to meet the needs of the subject and of different pupils;
- have knowledge and understanding of any statutory curriculum requirements for assessment, recording and reporting of pupils' attainment and progress;
- work with the SENCO and any other staff with special educational needs expertise, to ensure that individual education plans are used to set subject-specific targets and match work well to pupils' needs;
- establish and implement clear policies and practices for assessing, recording and reporting on pupil achievement, and for using this information to recognise achievement and to assist pupils in setting targets for further improvement;
- ensure that information about pupils' achievements in previous classes and schools is used effectively to secure good progress in the subject;
- monitor the progress made in achieving subject plans and targets, evaluate the effects on teaching and learning, and use this analysis to guide further improvement;
- evaluate the teaching of the subject in the school, use this analysis to identify effective practice and areas for improvement and take action to improve further the quality of teaching;
- establish clear targets for pupil achievement, and evaluate progress and achievement by all pupils, including those with special educational and linguistic needs.

According to OFSTED (2002a):[69]

Teachers are more comfortable teaching ICT skills to pupils and using literacy and numeracy work to practise and improve these skills rather than applying ICT skills to meet literacy or numeracy objectives. This distinction is quite often reflected by primary school timetables that give more emphasis to the development of ICT skills than application. Many schools use a systematic approach, often based on the Qualifications and Curriculum Authority scheme of work, to teach ICT skills, knowledge and understanding. However, teachers are much less clear when and when not to use ICT to support other subjects of the curriculum. Where teachers have good subject knowledge, and there is clear subject leadership and guidance, they are more able to decide on the appropriate use of ICT to enhance pupils' learning in literacy. Nevertheless, the application of ICT across the curriculum remains an uncertain area for many schools.

Planning for the effective use of ICT in all subjects

It has become quite usual in larger primary schools for teachers in the same year group to plan together, particularly for literacy and numeracy, but also where more than one class is studying the same topic, for example in history. This planning is likely to take place at the medium-term level, if not at the level of individual lessons – in many schools teachers work together to devise a weekly plan for literacy and numeracy.

Planning at all levels (short, medium and long term) should consider the use of ICT as a means of achieving the intended teaching and learning objectives for the subject. That is not, of course, to say that ICT should be used in every lesson – but decisions about whether or not to use it should be informed by a good understanding of the possibilities it presents. DfES Circular 4/98[33] and the NOF training guidance[82] have expected that teachers will have an awareness of when and when not to use ICT, and identify four particular functions of ICT that should be considered when deciding whether or not it would be appropriate. These are:

- speed and automatic functions;
- capacity and range;
- provisionality;
- interactivity.

Note that this list does not include:

- using ICT because children are motivated by it;
- using ICT because you know you are supposed to;
- using ICT as a reward for finishing other work.

To examine each in turn:

- *Speed and automatic functions* might include the ability of a database to search hundreds of records almost instantaneously, or a calculator to perform complex mathematical calculations, or a 'find and replace' function in a word processor to make alterations to a long document.
- *Capacity and range* might include having ready access to the sheer volume of material on the internet, or on CD-ROM encyclopaedias.
- *Provisionality* relates, for example, to the ease with which text or graphics can

be altered, and stored as a succession of drafts without the need to start from the beginning each time.

- *Interactivity* is a slightly more problematic concept. Much software and web material is described as interactive, which might mean no more than that the software can respond in different ways, depending on the choices the user makes. Human interactivity is of course more complex – when A talks to B, A can respond to B's reactions to what A is saying and modify what is said in order to agree with B or to make the explanation clearer. Computers are quite a long way away from being able to do that. However, there is a second sense in which interactivity may be a feature, in that it enables communication between people, for example by e-mail.

The implication is that if you examine your intended outcomes and cannot identify realistic ways in which ICT might be beneficial, then you should conclude that it would be inappropriate to use it. It does not follow that it must be used by everyone in the class, and you may well use it as a means of introducing differentiation into your lesson – but you must be sure that, over a period of time, everyone has reasonable access. You might find it desirable to discriminate somewhat in favour of the children who do not have access to a computer outside school.

Possible semi-legitimate reasons for not using ICT might include the following:

- No access to computer hardware, e.g. all the computers are in the computer suite and someone else is timetabled to use it. This was an inevitable consequence in schools where all the classroom machines were removed and placed in the computer suite. Despite the huge increase in the number of computers in primary schools, we are unlikely to reach the point where every child has access to their own computer all the time, at least in the foreseeable future. However, there are clear advantages to be had when classes have permanent access to at least one machine. Though the model of everyone taking a turn to use the classroom computer has not proved to be a very good one, there are still plenty of opportunities for effective use of a single computer by a group of children working collaboratively.

- The computer/monitor/printer is broken, and awaiting repair (see also Chapter 5). One of your functions as ICT co-ordinator is to make sure you are notified when this happens and to try to expedite the process of getting things fixed. If you operate under a managed service, this should not be too problematic. If the cost of repairs is seen as an inhibiting factor, draw your head teacher's attention to one of the numerous articles about the true cost of computer ownership. If you can (and if you have storage space), try and maintain a stock of spare equipment that can be used as a stop-gap in an emergency. This might include older machines that have been replaced but still work, albeit slowly. Treat these machines as stand-alones – it is probably unwise to try to hang them off the network, unless you have a thin-client system (discussion of which falls outside the scope of this book – if you have one, you will know what this means!).

- Appropriate software is not available. A very large part of what is really worth using ICT for in a primary classroom can be accomplished with the judicious use of relatively little generic software (a word processor, a database, a graphics program, etc.), though many teachers and classes have favourite pieces of subject-specific software.

Reasons for not using ICT should not include:

- I couldn't think of anything to do;
- I couldn't be bothered.

Support, enhance, transform

You should consider also how the use of ICT will affect what you do. You can use ICT to:

- *support* your lesson, to make it *easier*;
- *enhance* your lesson, to make it *better*;
- *transform* your lesson, to make it *different*.

The first two of these are relatively easy; to achieve the third you need to be bold.

Support

You can use ICT to support your teaching, for example by finding resources on the internet or by using a word processor to create a worksheet. It is possible to save some time this way, as:

- resources created can be stored electronically, and are reusable by other classes or by you next time you teach the same topic or unit; and
- because text files are provisional and malleable, it is relatively easy to create differentiated worksheets by creating one, saving it, modifying it, for example by simplifying the text, reducing the content, perhaps increasing the point size as appropriate, and re-saving under a different filename.

If your colleagues do not already know how, make a point of showing them how to cut and paste text from one file to another using keyboard shortcuts Ctrl-C and Ctrl-V. Show them how to copy pictures from the internet by clicking the right-hand button over an image and choosing Copy. Show them how to search for free clip art images via a search engine like Google[49] – it is often more immediately useful and productive to search on, say, *free clip art Romans* (or whatever) than to choose the Image Search and enter *Romans*, which almost always seems to generate irrelevance. This is a good example of the distinction between a skill and a technique, as explained in Chapter 6 – being shown those keyboard shortcuts takes no time or great effort; identifying the best way to frame your search question is a skill that can develop over time.

ICT has made the production of attractive worksheets far easier to accomplish (particularly for the less artistic) than it used to be. One thing you should consider, of course, is whether or not the creation of worksheets is in fact leading to good teaching.

There is no shortage of off-the-peg lesson plans available for download on the internet. If teaching were a more leisured pursuit, it would be easier to frown upon these and argue that teachers should always create their own lesson plans from scratch, so that they are directly relevant to the class being taught and so that they can be informed by assessment evidence from previous lessons. However, teachers are very hard-pressed, and keeping up with the paperwork can be a major headache. It may well be, then, that even highly conscientious, highly imaginative and creative teachers resort at least occasionally to off-the-peg plans. The trick, of course, is to customise them for your own use, to meet your own specific requirements. Teaching tends to be much more satisfactory when the teacher has a sense of ownership of the lesson.

Producing writing frames files on a word processor for children to complete the text might be an example of using ICT to support learning. If it is simply a matter of filling in the missing word, this is not necessarily any different from what you might have done as a paper-based exercise.

A key characteristic of the use of ICT to support your lesson is that it is still essentially the same lesson that you might have planned if ICT had not been available.

Enhance

Your use of ICT may enable you to enhance your teaching and make it better, for example by using the internet to enable children to use resources to which they would not previously have had access, or by using PowerPoint to present a series of slides to convey factual information about a topic in a structured yet lively way, or by using an online big book as a shared reading activity, or by using a simple painting program to create a greetings card. The essential feature here is that what is being done could all have been done without the use of a computer, though it might not have been as effective.

Transform

Your lesson is transformed when you are enabled to do something that was not possible without the use of ICT. This might include children creating a multimedia presentation or web page as an outcome of research done for a history topic, taking part in an international online survey via e-mail, designing and building a burglar alarm using sensors and control equipment, creating a short animated sequence using models and a digital camera, or making a talking story. A large proportion of worthwhile ICT activity in this category provides children with scope to participate as resourceful, collaborative learners.

Teaching with ICT – what does good practice look like?

The NAACE discussion document (NAACE, 2001)[57] identifies five key features of effective practice in the use of ICT:

- Autonomy
  - *Pupils develop autonomy through their use of ICT. They take control of their learning. They engage with the technology and work independently or with others, at the most effective pace and at the most appropriate level. They articulate reasons for their use of ICT.*

- Capability
  - *Pupils are developing good ICT skills that they deploy appropriately to the task in hand, with increasing confidence and competence.*
  - *Pupils transfer and apply their skills using ICT effectively to support learning in other subjects.*
  - *Pupils experiment purposefully, problem solving through extrapolating from previous experience.*
  - *Pupils develop the ability to make critical judgements about the contribution of ICT to their work and understand the value of using ICT.*

- Creativity
  - *Pupils are inspired to be creative with ICT.*
  - *Pupils release their creative ability through a range of ICT tools.*
  - *Pupils use ICT to explore styles of communication and expression.*
  - *Pupils are innovative/creative in their use of ICT.*
  - *Pupils explore the possibilities of multimedia tools, enabling them to create in the styles readily available to them in games, CDs and television.*

- Quality
  - *Pupils use ICT to present and communicate their ideas to a high standard, redrafting as necessary to produce better quality outcomes.*
  - *Pupils have clear ideas of how they use ICT to improve the quality of their work.*
  - *Pupils readily engage in thinking about the task in hand. They explain what they have done and why. They justify their use of ICT in terms of the quality of the outcomes.*
  - *Pupils display evident pride and satisfaction. They value the outcomes of their endeavours. They develop a personal commitment to good quality work and aspire to the highest standards.*
  - *Pupils have high expectations and demonstrate concentration, persistence and determination to develop work of a high standard.*
  - *Pupils are engaged in high quality thinking and analysis through decision-making, predicting, hypothesising and testing.*

- Scope
  - *Pupils employ ICT to gain access to experiences, information or resources in ways that are not possible with other media. This extends opportunities and brings a new dimension to teaching and learning.*

– Pupils' learning is enhanced by reaching beyond the classroom, via e-mail, internet use etc., expanding their knowledge and understanding of the world.
– Pupils use ICT to think in new ways. Pupils use ICT to explore and question, hypothesise and predict. They find different ways to do things.

The document provides classroom examples to illustrate each of these features, spread across a range of year groups. There is insufficient space here to explore these in detail; the document is recommended reading for any intending ICT co-ordinator.

Reflection

Consider your own practice, and that of other teachers you have observed. How many of the above characteristics do you think are present in your classroom, or in theirs?

Having read the above, how will you try develop your own practice? How will you try to advise your colleagues?

Meeting individual needs and promoting inclusion

You will have some responsibility for ensuring that ICT is used appropriately to support children with a variety of needs. These might include disabilities, for example:

- general learning difficulties;
- a specific learning difficulty, e.g. with language;
- emotional and behavioural difficulties;
- physical disabilities;
- hearing impairment;
- visual impairment;

or other issues which make a child's needs different from those of other children, for example:

- very high ability;
- an ability or talent in a particular area, e.g. music;
- health problems which make full-time attendance at school difficult.

In most cases, you might need to work in concert with the SENCO to determine an appropriate course of action or what appropriate adaptations might need to be made. Your school should be particularly aware of the implications of the Disability Discrimination Act 1995, and you will need to make sure that ICT facilities are accessible by all – for example, it would be unwise to locate your computer room in an upstairs classroom if it is not accessible to wheelchair users.

- Supportive software like word processors with speech facilities, word banks and spellcheckers can enable communication for children for whom writing is problematic. Voice recognition software can also be useful in some contexts.

- A whole range of adapted input devices is available, including switches, trackerballs, touch screens and large keyboards, for children with poor fine motor co-ordination.

- Children with visual impairment can make use of the internet by means of software which reads pages to them. If you are responsible for your school website, make sure it complies with accessibility requirements.

- Very able children can make use of ICT as a source of enrichment materials. See, for example, the NRICH mathematics site.[66]

- Children with emotional and behavioural difficulties can very often be positively motivated by the use of ICT. Teachers often report that children whose attention span is normally very limited can concentrate for greater lengths of time when working at a computer.

Your LEA will probably provide support for children with special needs, and should in some cases provide extra equipment to individuals to enable them to access the curriculum. Make sure you establish a clear understanding regarding responsibility for the maintenance of this equipment.

There is plenty of good advice available about ICT for inclusion. Start with that provided by BECTa.[4]

Making the best use of classroom assistants

One of the most significant changes in the primary school in recent years has been the rapid expansion in the number of classroom assistants. Those who are designated as learning support assistants may be allocated to work with particular children for all or most of their time, to enable those children to access as much of the curriculum as possible. In some cases, this will automatically have an ICT dimension, as the children with whom they work may have specialised equipment available to them. It is fairly common for classroom assistants to work with groups of children within, say, the Literacy Hour. In quite a few schools, they are expected to work with groups of children using computers. Go out of your way to make friends with them, as they are potentially your allies, and they might make your life easier. Obviously, it helps if they already have some basic ICT skills.

- An audit of their existing skills may reveal substantial unrecognised experience or potential.

- Make sure they are familiar with the software in common use in the classes with which they work, and that they understand the educational value of it.

- If they are working with individual children, make sure they are completely conversant with the functions of any access devices the children may be using.

- In particular, ensure that they support and scaffold children's work appropriately, by questioning and prompting, and not by doing the work for them.

- Wherever possible, include them in any ICT staff development sessions – though you may need to clarify how they will be remunerated for this.

- If possible, try to work closely with one or two people to try to develop their ICT troubleshooting skills – this is where your time can be substantially saved in the longer term.

Assessment through observation

Outside the confines of the whole-class ICT lesson, it is very tempting to use the computer as a childminder while you work with other groups or individuals and not particularly pay attention to what children are actually doing. As long as they are engrossed and not visibly squabbling, complete the task, or save and print out their work, why intervene? There are several reasons:

- The computer is not actually listening to the children or making judgements about how decisions are reached, whether or not all members of the group are participating actively or whether the apparent collective understanding of the group is in fact the understanding of one or two dominant members.

- If children are engaged in a drill-and-practice activity and get something wrong, the computer has no insight into how or why they got it wrong. Similarly, it cannot detect whether a correct response is the result of careful reasoning and collective agreement or whether it is a blind guess.

- One of the most important skills of the outstanding teacher lies in identifying key questions to ask when children are stuck, or even while they appear to be progressing satisfactorily, knowing how to phrase those questions for maximum effectiveness and knowing how to supplement them in the light of children's responses.

- For assessment purposes, merely seeing the printout at the end tells you relatively little about the processes that children actually employed, and whether, for example, there were some misconceptions or limited understandings embedded in them that could have been corrected through direct intervention (for example centring a heading by repeatedly pressing the space bar). Really effective assessment entails consideration of *process* at least as much as *product*.

Assessment and record-keeping

Ask yourself the following questions about record-keeping for assessment purposes:

- Who is responsible for the records that are kept?

  - Obviously, class teachers are responsible for records they keep of children's activities, achievements, progress, misconceptions or areas in need of further support. On the other hand, there is a great deal to be said for involving children in their own assessment, and this might include, for example, each child maintaining a folder of printouts, evaluation sheets and other evidence as an individual ICT portfolio. The level of sophistication of this portfolio will probably depend on the age of the children in the class. Children evaluating and reflecting upon their own performance are learning to become independent learners, and the process of maintaining a portfolio should help to develop their metacognitive awareness. It should not become an onerous chore, however, or it may well become counter-productive.

- Where are records kept?
  - If assessment information is to be used formatively, to inform short-term planning, the records need to be maintained close at hand, in the classroom.

- What information is being recorded?
  - Bear in mind the distinction made earlier between a skill and a technique. If the general approach to assessment recording in your school is in favour of tick-lists of skills, then go along with this, but try not to atomise it into lists of the 'can make text bold...can make text italic' type. That is profoundly uninteresting and can mask the real questions about the development of the types of understanding and skills described in the National Curriculum Programme of Study (see Chapter 6). Rather, after a re-drafting exercise, record 'understands how word processors can support the efficient redrafting of text', and if possible support this with evidence. Annotated printouts can be a useful way of doing this – remember that a large part of what is actually worth assessing is to do with *process* rather than *product*. Your annotations can remind you, or others, of the context in which the work was produced, and anything specifically noteworthy about its production.
  - Record information about ICT achievement not only from within generic ICT lessons, but also from occasions when ICT has been used across the curriculum.
  - Another piece of information you should seek to record is what you know about individuals' ICT activities outside school. Do they have access to a computer at home? If so, what do they use it for? If children have well-developed skills that have not been specifically taught at school, how will you account for these when making judgements about what ICT tasks you will expect children to undertake?

- In what format/s should it be recorded?
  - Most teachers have a system for recording which children have completed which tasks. If they do not already do this or something similar, you might encourage your colleagues to set up as a template a standard word-processed table, containing a number of columns. The first column contains the names of all the children in the class (and perhaps on similar pages, the names arranged by maths group, literacy group or whatever – let the power of provisionality work for you!), with spaces at the top of the page for you to insert the date, subject, and focus of the particular task undertaken, and perhaps a box in which you can add any other general notes. At the head of each of the next columns (perhaps three, four or five of them) leave space to add headings for the particular objective, skill or understanding being assessed. Keep the right-hand column reasonably wide. Save this template. For each activity in which you are recording assessment information, produce a separate class list. You can either write on it by hand or else enter your information directly at the computer.

Use whatever system you prefer to record the basic information about who did what – there are many variations on this, including triangles or stars or different coloured dots. Use the right-hand column to record significant achievement by individuals or particular points to note if children are having difficulties.

- Do not feel obliged to fill in a comment for every child on every occasion – much of that information will never be of specific use to anyone.
- You may want to add supporting evidence, like printouts, or you may prefer to entrust these to children's individual portfolios.
- Portfolios should obviously include printouts, but could also include self-assessment sheets of the '*I can...*' variety. For younger children these might be little more than a few printed words with some smileys or balloons (or whatever) to colour in. For older children, encourage them to record some evidence, stating how they know they have achieved the objective.
- When you come to form a summative judgement of each child's achievement, it is easier and far more instructive to do this by looking at the portfolio than it is by looking at a set of tick-lists.
- You might record assessment information electronically via a spreadsheet or dedicated 'assessment' software, but if you do so, keep in mind the above comments.

- Who will have access to the information?

  - The children have their portfolios, and you have your record book. Portfolios should be very useful at parents' evenings, and some might be used in staff meetings where moderation or 'levelling' takes place and the school portfolio is updated (see below). You might also wish to extract one or two typical pieces of work (preferably annotated) to place in individual children's records.

- What will the information be used for?

  - Assessment information collected should be used formatively to help you plan what to do next, and summatively to make overall judgements of children's achievements at the end of the year. If it is doing neither job, why keep it?

Maintaining a school portfolio of ICT evidence

There should be a school portfolio of ICT evidence to identify the school's understanding of what represents different levels of attainment within the National Curriculum. A large part of the content of this may well be drawn partly from work done in timetabled ICT sessions, perhaps giving examples of outcomes from units in the QCA Scheme of Work, but you should also consciously try to include examples of children's work done in other subjects where ICT has been used.

Two good starting places for this activity are the QCA National Curriculum in Action website,[75] which gives many examples of children's work with lesson details and individual commentaries, and the Northern Grid electronic portfolio[65] which gives examples of children's work for each National Curriculum level, with a commentary detailing how each level varies from, and is a development from, the level below. If you can arrange it, present material from these sites at a staff meeting or staff development session, ask teachers to comment on it, then ask them to present work from their own classes for comparison and conduct a moderation exercise. They should then select examples to be indicative of each level, including pieces which only just merit a particular level and also pieces which almost merit a higher level. This will help the staff as a whole to gain a clear understanding of the characteristics of each level.

When you retain the material as a portfolio (either paper-based or in electronic form, or preferably both), you should be careful to include details of the context in which the work was completed. The portfolio should be updated, perhaps every two years, to reflect the ways in which ICT has developed. You will probably wish to conduct this exercise in tandem with the assessment co-ordinator. The purpose of the portfolio is to present a consistent picture of the development of ICT capability. In practice, the process of 'levelling' might serve to chivvy any recalcitrant or complacent members of the teaching staff, but try not to let the exercise make the less confident teachers feel threatened.

Monitoring the use of ICT in teaching

You may be approached by colleagues who say, *'I've got to teach something with spreadsheets today, and I'm not very confident with them. Would you like to swap classes? I'll take yours for PE...'*

However much you may prefer spreadsheets to PE, and however much the arrangement might appear to be beneficial to both classes, the short answer is no. If you set precedents, you could find yourself doing a lot of ICT-based teaching in other people's classrooms, which might be an appealing prospect for you (being the One Who Knows), but it does nothing to foster the general sense of ICT competence that should pervade your school, and in some senses it can actually deskill your colleagues. A much better idea is to seek extra cover for your own class and offer to work alongside the other teacher, either demonstrating or else providing help and reassurance wherever it is needed. If your head teacher is really keen to promote ICT within the school, requests of that nature should be looked upon favourably, as long as they are not too frequent. Try to find space after such lessons to discuss them with your colleagues. Teachers have ZPDs too – they should aim to be able to do the same thing unaided next time.

Similarly, if you can manage to observe your colleagues when they are teaching, either in the computer room or else in their own classrooms in a relatively ICT-intensive lesson, this will help you to maintain an overall picture of the general state of ICT teaching in the school. Of course, take note of the evidence of achievement in children's work on the walls etc., but remember that you should be evaluating process at least as much as product. Try to ensure that such observations are planned, relate to staff development issues identified elsewhere and are seen as supportive rather than intrusive.

Summary

Lesson planning across the curriculum should consider when and when not to use ICT, in terms of speed and automatic functions, capacity and range, provisionality and interactivity. ICT can support lessons to make them easier, enhance lessons to make them better or transform lessons to make them different. According to NAACE the five features that characterise good practice in the use of ICT are autonomy, capability, creativity, quality and scope. ICT is a very good means of promoting inclusion and of meeting individual needs.

Assessment of ICT should take account of process as well as product, and children should be encouraged to keep an ICT portfolio as a means of self-assessment. This could provide the raw material when the school ICT portfolio is updated. You should monitor the work of your colleagues by working alongside them if possible.

9 HOME, SCHOOL AND THE WIDER COMMUNITY

(→) According to the National Standards for Subject Leadership, you should:

- ensure effective development of pupils' individual and collaborative study skills necessary for them to become increasingly independent when out of school;

- establish a partnership with parents to involve them in their child's learning of the subject, as well as providing information about curriculum, attainment, progress and targets;

- develop effective links with the local community, including business and industry, in order to extend the subject, enhance teaching and develop the pupils' wider understanding.

The middle letter in ICT stands for communication (or communications...). It is obviously then your business to consider ways in which the school communicates with the outside world, both in terms of the promulgation of ICT and more generally. Bear in mind also that communication is a two-way process. It is not simply a matter of telling the rest of the world what you are doing; it is equally a matter of being receptive to what the rest of the world has to offer, or what it thinks about what you are doing; it is also about establishing and sustaining dialogue.

In this regard, you should consider:

- how to co-ordinate ICT activity that takes place both at school and at home;
- the implications of the digital divide;
- how you keep parents informed about school policy and practice in ICT;
- what links you might fruitfully develop with local businesses and the community at large;
- relations with children, schools or other agencies outside the immediate environment of your school;
- what safeguards need to operate in order to make the process of communication as unproblematic as possible.

According to a survey conducted for the DfES,[44] in the UK in 2002:

- 81 per cent of households with children of school age had a computer by comparison with 78 per cent in 2001;

- internet access in those households rose from 64 per cent to 68 per cent in the same period;

- 45 per cent of 3–4-year-olds made use of their parents' computers;

- 64 per cent of Key Stage 1 children and 74 per cent of Key Stage 2 children used a computer at home;

- of those children who did not have access to a computer at home, almost all had access to one at someone else's house;

- the proportion of Key Stage 2 children who used computers to do homework rose from 7 per cent in 2001 to 40 per cent in 2002;

- the most commonly cited reason for having a computer at home was to support children's school work;

- 56 per cent of primary children who had access to a home computer were considered to be functioning at an intermediate, advanced or expert level, by comparison with 33 per cent of those who did not have access to a computer at home.

We will soon have reached the point where computers are as much a part of the expected contents of a home as televisions or refrigerators. What is being made abundantly clear by the survey quoted above, and by research projects such as Screen Play[46] and ImpaCT2[15] is that children spend more time using a computer outside school than they do in school, that they develop a range of ICT skills that are not always recognised or allowed for in schools' ICT planning, and that there is, at least among older children, a steadily growing level of frustration with the ICT opportunities provided by schools. We now hear stories of children e-mailing their class work to themselves at home because they have better equipment there.

Some commentators read into this the end of school as we know it, with children participating in online virtual schooling from remote locations. Though a good case might be made for looking at the possibilities of asynchronous communication (for example through a conferencing system) as a means of supporting a rich and varied learning environment in the upper years of the primary school, there are a number of overriding factors which will determine that the days of the primary school are not numbered at all. The first, and most obvious, is the duty of care, which every teacher accepts. A second is the belief, profoundly held by probably all primary teachers, that school serves a vital function in children's social education. A third is that although so many children have access to a computer and the internet at home, there are still quite a few who do not. The issue of the 'digital divide' is one that will need to be addressed.[18]

What you will have to try to ensure is that ICT experiences in school do not become disappointing by comparison with what is available at home. This does not mean that children should spend their days playing arcade games, though there is a growing interest in looking at what the games and 'edutainment' industry might have to offer the world of education. Certainly it is clear that children can be engrossed in a computer game in a way and to a depth that they rarely muster in the context of school work. See, for example, the BECTa discussion.[7]

If you work with children in Key Stage 2, you should be aware of GridClub,[50] which is a website supported by the DfES among others. It is free for users, and is specifically designed to be a safe online environment for children between the ages of 7 and 11, that is equally useable in a school context and a home context. In order to achieve this, it has to appeal to three different constituencies simultaneously, and persuade:

- teachers that it is educational;
- parents that it is safe;
- children that it is cool.

It manages to do this by including a wide range of lively educational games (of perhaps rather uneven quality) and useful resources like a very child-friendly dictionary and an atlas, and particularly through its chat rooms. In order to participate in these, users must be within the Key Stage 2 age range and registration can only be done through schools. The range of discussion groups includes the themes that predictably attract children (football, bands), but also a wider range of hobbies and interests. Discussions are mediated by an adult at all times, so inappropriate contributions can be filtered and offenders warned or barred.

All children should have their own e-mail addresses. If it is your policy to issue and manage these via the school, bear in mind that many children already have their own e-mail addresses. If you set up a system that enables auto-forwarding of messages, this should also help the development of home–school links, particularly as the proportion of people with broadband connections continues to rise.

So far very few schools have made significant progress in setting up effective home–school links to manage a two-way flow of information for parents and children. It should be possible to establish some means by which details of homework assignments and so forth can be transmitted electronically. One way of doing this would be to establish a school intranet, which is a local network, located within the school, to which outside users can gain access via a password. Another way would be by means of a conferencing system.

Publicise the work of the Parents Information Network (PIN), whose website[71] contains evaluations of good quality software for the home, sound advice on suitable websites, and clear and authoritative guidance on a range of issues to do with the use of ICT in the home, including how to use ICT to support homework. They have a section specifically for parents of 5–7-year-olds. PIN design courses, to be delivered in schools by anyone (which may or may not mean you...) to develop parents' ICT skills, and to show them how to support their children's learning with ICT. The website also provides a button which you can place on your school website to link to theirs.

A similar source of ICT materials for the home is the DfES Parents Online site,[35] which has links to a wide range of sites, arranged by age or topic – including links to websites for parents to use with under-fives.

Parents wishing to know more about the place of ICT in education, and how they can help and support their children, could be directed to the BECTa Information Sheet, *Parents, ICT and Education*,[16] which contains a number of links to other resources.

Your ICT development plan commits you to considering how to make your ICT facilities available to parents and others – you should also consider to what extent your school website is a two-way communication with parents and the wider community. What mutual benefit might be derived from providing a link on your school website for local businesses, sports teams, community facilities, arts and entertainment facilities, clubs and societies, particularly if you provide some reason for parents to access the site regularly?

Summary

Home ownership of computers has increased rapidly, and it is now not possible to ignore children's substantial use of ICT outside school. This raises some issues that will need to be thought through in terms of ensuring that the ICT curriculum meets everyone's needs, from the precocious experts to those on the far side of the digital divide. Parents should be encouraged to support their children's use of ICT for educational purposes, and links between home and school, e.g. via e-mail, should be strengthened. Relations with other sectors of the community can also be enhanced by means of ICT.

10 CONCLUSION

This book began with a brief look at the path that has led us to the current position, and it will finish with a glance at possible paths that lie ahead. One thing that is certain is that the pace of technological change will not slow up, and the equipment we are using today will eventually look as quaint as an epidiascope or a spirit duplicator.

Future-gazing in the world of education is a precarious process. Cuban (1986)[30] presented quotations from various periods of the twentieth century confidently predicting the radical transformation of education at the hands of film, or radio, or television, and showed that each of these media failed to do so for basically the same reasons – that education is not simply a technical process, and that the technologies were solutions to problems that teachers did not perceive themselves as having.

The history of computers in education is similarly littered with red herrings and blind alleys. It is interesting that schools and classrooms of the future, as portrayed in future-gazing presentations and videos, always seem to have enormous amounts of space, are unnaturally clean and tidy, and seem to have very small teaching groups.

However, some technological innovations will inevitably have a major impact on the way teaching and learning develops. The DfES document *Transforming The Way We Learn*[42] identifies, among other things:

- greater portability of computers, perhaps with wireless networking;
- the development of school intranets which can be accessed from home by pupils, teachers and parents via the internet;
- an increase in the use in school of ICT brought from home by children and teachers;
- broadband communications;
- developments in presentation technologies (for example interactive whiteboards), digital video and the publishing of children's work online;
- greater use of, for example, voice-activated software by children with special needs to increase their access to the curriculum.

In thinking about developments like these, you would be wise to keep in mind the workings of the Technological Imperative. This is the unwritten rule that seems to state that because it is technically possible to do something, that is what you should do. Schools are fundamentally conservative places, and as the ICT co-ordinator you are likely to be the person identified with technological change. Sometimes you will find yourself needing to justify this to sceptical colleagues. Make sure that you are able to do so on grounds of good pedagogy – learning and teaching will not be transformed by new technologies unless the change can be justified in educational terms. Teachers have proved very adept at subverting innovation, and turning it into a version of what they were doing anyway.

Wireless networking is already beginning to have an impact. At present, as we have seen in Chapter 7, this is still slightly tentative, and the wireless systems can struggle to keep pace with whole classes attempting to access the network simultaneously, but the pace of technological advance will make this an efficient way of doing things in the very near future. At that point, schools can reconsider whether or not they really need a dedicated computer room. If space is not at a premium, there may be good reason to retain a central and well-equipped area to which classes can go when they need to use ICT simultaneously, and also to retain a location where after-school ICT activity can take place, including, for example, evening classes for parents. On the other hand, schools may decide that it is time they reclaimed their library or music room.

Another significant change, which is closely related to the rise of the wireless network, is a gradual drift towards the use of laptops and other small portable devices. Again, as we have seen, there are potential problems over battery life, but the amount of space required by a laptop computer is so small by comparison with a desktop machine that it seems to make good sense, and the sheer portability of laptops means that the computer can be taken to the learning, rather than having to take the learning to the computer.

The vast majority of exhibitors at shows like BETT now use flat-screen monitors. As the price of these continues to fall, we should eventually witness the disappearance of the cathode ray tube and smaller monitor sizes, even on desktop machines, mean more space for books and other equipment.

Eventually, we may well see very large touch-sensitive flat screens at universally affordable prices. When that happens, the functionality now provided by a data projector and interactive whiteboard will be significantly simplified, and the use of data projectors could be limited to functions that require their portability. There are some significant advantages to be had here – at present data projectors are expensive, replacement bulbs are exorbitantly priced, and, even when the projector is ceiling-mounted, users find they are working in their own shadow.

It is now quite normal for schools to have digital cameras, and for children of any age to be expected – and allowed – operate them. One new area which is making rapid progress as prices become more affordable is the use of digital video. This is already making a huge impact in secondary schools in curriculum areas like PE or performing arts, where pupils' performances can be captured and replayed instantly, or else edited quickly to provide a permanent record or portfolio of what was done. This is an area in which Apple computers currently excel, as *iMovie* software is included on almost all new computers. This software makes video editing so simple and quick that it becomes a realistic thing to expect children to do, certainly across Key Stage 2. Giving children scope to create their own video presentations is potentially an enormously creative use of the technology. Those who have done it will readily attest to the very high levels of on-task activity and the high-quality collaboration and teamwork it engenders. BECTa have initiated Creativity in Digital Video awards, for which children of all ages are eligible.[9]

Digital video requires huge quantities of memory and storage space. Increasingly, as a few more twists of Moore's Law gives us computers and other devices with sufficient storage capacity to cope with the multiple gigabytes that digital video can consume, and as it becomes normal for schools to have broadband communications, the ability to transmit and receive video materials in real time may have a profound effect on the way we work in the classroom.

Videoconferencing is an area which has been talked and written about for several years, and which has been employed by a few enthusiasts in primary schools, but which has not yet really 'taken off'. Two possible reasons that suggest themselves are:

- There is not much to do with videoconferencing that is really worth doing in the primary curriculum at present. So far the use of videoconferencing has had more to do with the Technological Imperative than it has to do with perceived primary pedagogy. It is nice to be able to converse with children in other places, 'live' via a video link, but it is not something that most teachers would identify as a high priority, or something that they would wish to do with sufficient frequency to justify the expense.

- The technology is not yet good enough to justify its use or to keep people enthusiastic about doing it. The quality of image received, and the frequency with which systems seem to break down, have discouraged all but a few early adopters. This is about to change, as it becomes more normal for people to be able to send and receive video images via their mobile phones.

Quite possibly, the best uses of videoconferencing have not been thought of yet. The anticipated expansion of modern foreign languages within the primary curriculum may provide a justification for its rapid development.

There is quite a lot that is uncertain at present about the way new technologies will affect the way primary education operates. On the one hand you need to be aware of the implications of research such as Screen Play[46] and ImpaCT2,[15] which clearly indicate that children spend more time engaging with new technologies outside school than they do in school; on the other hand, as we have seen, whatever form the e-learning revolution takes, it is unlikely to bring about the demise of primary schools as we know them. As an ICT co-ordinator, when you think about the future you should consider:

- what is technically possible;
- what is educationally desirable;
- what is currently workable in your school.

Keeping those three things in mind is like trying to juggle three balls that are not necessarily following the same trajectory. It is a fascinating and sometimes awesome task.

This section lists the paper-based references in the book, and also the web addresses (URLs) referred to in the text. The complete set of hyperlinks is available from the Learning Matters website: **www.learningmatters.co.uk/education**.

Once there, you will need to do a search for *Successful ICT Leadership in Primary Schools* to locate this associated resource.

There is, of course, no guarantee that all the links provided here will continue to be available indefinitely. All links were checked and known to be working at the end of March 2003.

1. Aion Needlecrafts: *UK Stitching Sites List*
   www.aion-needlecrafts.co.uk/sssi/sssi.htm

2. Alliance for Childhood: *Fool's Gold: A Critical Look at Computers in Childhood*
   www.allianceforchildhood.net/projects/computers/computers_reports.htm

3. BBC: *Schools: Ages 4–11*
   www.bbc.co.uk/schools/4_11/

4. BECTa: *An Overview of Special Educational Needs and ICT Provision*
   www.ictadvice.org.uk/index.php?section=tl&cat=002002&rid=1955

5. BECTa: *Building the Grid: ICT Development Planning*
   buildingthegrid.becta.org.uk/index.php?locid=130

6. BECTa: *Building the Grid: Job Descriptions and ICT Support Staff*
   buildingthegrid.becta.org.uk/index.php?locid=164

7. BECTa: *Computer Games in Education*
   www.becta.org.uk/research/reports/cge.cfm

8. *BECTa: Connecting Schools, Networking People 2002*
   www.becta.org.uk/publications/connecting.html

9. BECTa: *Creativity in Digital Video Awards*
   www.becta.org.uk/creativityawards/

10. BECTa: *Designing Computer Suites and Workstations in Schools*
    buildingthegrid.becta.org.uk/docs/ict_design.pdf

11. BECTa: *ENI and SETT Online Conference: ICT in Schools Across the UK*
    forum.ngfl.gov.uk/webx/eni-settconference

12. BECTa: *How Do I Write School ICT Policies and ICT Development Plans?*
    www.becta.org.uk/start/ictplans.html

13. BECTa: *How to Conduct a School ICT Audit*
    www.ictadvice.org.uk/index.php?section=ap&cat=004001&rid=434

14. BECTa: *How to Ensure the Safe Use of ICT in Schools*
    www.ictadvice.org.uk/index.php?section=te&cat=001000&rid=151

15. BECTa: *ICT Research: ImpaCT2*
    www.becta.org.uk/research/reports/impact2/index.cfm

16. BECTa: *Parents, ICT and Education*
    www.becta.org.uk/technology/infosheets/html/parents.html

17. BECTa: *Technical Paper: Firewalls*
    www.ictadvice.org.uk/downloads/whatis/firewalls_tech.doc

18. BECTa: *The Digital Divide*
    www.becta.org.uk/research/reports/digidivide.cfm

19. BECTa: *What Are the Management Issues of Creating a School Web Site?*
    www.ictadvice.org.uk/index.php?section=te&cat=008003&rid=193

20. BECTa: *What Is a Firewall?*
    www.ictadvice.org.uk/index.php?section=te&cat=007000&rid=625

21. BECTa: *What Is a Primary School ICT Policy?*
    www.ictadvice.org.uk/index.php?section=ap&cat=004000&rid=174

22. BECTa: *What Is an Acceptable Use Policy?*
    www.ictadvice.org.uk/index.php?section=ap&cat=004002&rid=463

23. BECTa: *What Is an ICT Scheme of Work?*
    www.ictadvice.org.uk/index.php?section=tl&cat=004000&rid=443

24. BECTa: *What Is Broadband?*
    www.ictadvice.org.uk/index.php?section=te&cat=008000&rid=1796

26. BECTa: *What Is Foundation Stage ICT?*
    www.ictadvice.org.uk/index.php?section=tl&cat=001000&rid=630

27. BECTa: *What Is ICT?*
    www.ictadvice.org.uk/index.php?section=tl&cat=001001006&rid=1701

28. BECTa: *What Makes a Good ICT Development Plan?*
    www.ictadvice.org.uk/index.php?section=ap&cat=004000&rid=2154

29. BECTa/The Guardian: *UK Education Web Site Awards: Effective Web Design*
    www.becta.org.uk/schools/websiteawards/effectivedesign.html

30. Cuban, L. (1986) *Teachers and Machines: The Classroom Use of Technology since 1920.*
    New York: Teachers College Press.

31. Devon Curriculum Services: *Information and Communication Technology*
    www.devon.gov.uk/dcs/ict/index.html

32. DfES: *Curriculum Online*
    www.curriculumonline.gov.uk/

33. DfES (1998) *Initial Teacher Training Curriculum for the Use of Information and
    Communications Technology in Subject Teaching* (Circular 4/98)
    www.dfes.gov.uk/publications/guidanceonthelaw/4_98/annexb.htm

34. DfES: *Parents' Centre*
    www.dfes.gov.uk/parents/

35. DfES: *Parents Online*
    www.parentsonline.gov.uk/

36. DfES (1999) *Statistics of Education: Survey of Information and Communications Technology in Schools 1999*
    www.dfes.gov.uk/statistics/DB/SBU/b0125/76x-05.htm

37. DfES (2002) *Statistics of Education: Survey of Information and Communications Technology in Schools 2002*
    www.dfes.gov.uk/statistics/DB/SBU/b0360/sb07-2002.pdf

38. DfES: *Superhighway Safety: Safe Use of the Internet*
    safety.ngfl.gov.uk/schools/

39. DfES: *Superhighway Safety: Safe Use of the Internet at Home and at School*
    safety.ngfl.gov.uk/parents/

40. DfES: *Superhighway Safety: Images of Pupils on School Web Sites*
    safety.ngfl.gov.uk/schools/document.php3?D=d27

41. DfES (1999) *Teachers' Standards Framework: Helping You Develop*
    www.dfes.gov.uk/teachers/professional_development

42. DfES (2002) *Transforming the Way We Learn*
    www.dfes.gov.uk/ictfutures/

43. DfES/QCA: *National Curriculum Online*
    www.nc.uk.net/home.html

44. DfES: *Young People and ICT 2002*
    www.becta.org.uk/research/reports/youngpeopleict/full_report.pdf

45. Disney: *Cybernetiquette Comix*
    disney.go.com/cybersafety/

46. Facer, K., Furlong, J., Furlong, R., and Sutherland, R. (2001) *Screen Play Project: Summary of Results and Publications*. Bristol University.
    www.bris.ac.uk/Depts/Education/finalsummary.doc

47. Fox, R. (2002) 'The ICT Audit: Self-Reporting of ICT Skills by Primary Undergraduates, 1998–2001', ITTE Research Conference, Cambridge (unpublished research paper).

48. Freedman, T. (1999) *Managing ICT*. London: Hodder & Stoughton.

49. *Google*
    www.google.com

50. *GridClub*
    www.gridclub.com/

51. *Infant Explorer*
    www.naturegrid.org.uk/infant/

52. *Kartoo*
    www.kartoo.com

53. Kent CC: *Schools Internet Policy 2001*
    www.kented.org.uk/ngfl/policy.html

54. MAPE
    www.mape.org.uk

55. McKenzie, J. (1999) *Reaching the Reluctant Teacher*
staffdevelop.org/reluctant.html

56. Moore, G.A. (1991) *Crossing the Chasm*. New York: HarperCollins.

57. NAACE (2002) *Characteristics of Good Teaching and Learning*
www.naace.org.uk/resourceView.asp?menuitemid=2&resourceid= 47

58. NAACE (2003) *Implementing ICT*
www.naace.org.uk/resourceView.asp?menuitemid=2&resourceid= 310

59. NAACE: *Tool to Determine the ICT Co-ordinator's Role*
www.naace.org/impict/resources/Prioritising_the%20ICT_coordinators_role.doc

60. *Net Nanny*
www.netnanny.com/

61. NGfL: *Grid Watch*
www.ngfl.gov.uk/about_ngfl/gridwatch.jsp?sec=20

62. NGfL: *KidSmart*
www.kidsmart.org.uk/

63. NGfL: *Laptops for Teachers*
lft.ngfl.gov.uk/

64. NGfL: *The National Grid for Learning*
www.ngfl.gov.uk/

65. Northern Grid: *ICT Electronic Portfolio*
www.northerngrid.org/ngflwebsite/ep.htm

66. NRICH: *Online Maths Club*
www.nrich.maths.org.uk/

67. OFSTED (2001) *ICT in Schools: The Impact of Government Initiatives – Interim Report*
www.ofsted.gov.uk/publications/docs/1043.pdf

68. OFSTED (2002a) *ICT in Schools: Effects of Government Initiatives*
www.ofsted.gov.uk/publications/docs/19.pdf

69. OFSTED (2002b) *ICT in Schools: Effect of Government Initiatives – Implementation in Primary Schools and Effect on Literacy*
www.ofsted.gov.uk/publications/docs/2615.pdf

70. Papert, S. (1980) *Mindstorms: Children, Computers and Powerful Ideas*. London: Harvester Wheatsheaf.

71. Parents Information Network
www.pin.org.uk/

72. QCA (1998) *Information Technology: A Scheme of Work for Key Stages 1 and 2*. London: DfEE/QCA.
www.standards.dfes.gov.uk/schemes/it/

73. QCA (2001) *Curriculum Guidance for the Foundation Stage*. London: QCA.
www.qca.org.uk/ca/foundation/guidance/curr_guidance.asp

74. QCA (2002) *Designing and Timetabling the Primary Curriculum: A Practical Guide for Key Stages 1 and 2*
   www.qca.org.uk/ca/5-14/learning_prim_curr.asp

75. QCA: *National Curriculum in Action: ICT Home Page*
   www.ncaction.org.uk/subjects/ict/

76. Rogers, E.M. (1995) *The Diffusion of Innovations*, 3rd edn. New York: Free Press.

77. Skinner, B.F. (1968) *The Technology of Teaching*. New York: Appleton-Century-Crofts.

78. Stevenson, D. *et al.* (1997) *Information and Communication Technology in UK Schools: An Independent Enquiry*. London: ICT in Schools Commission.
   rubble.ultralab.anglia.ac.uk/stevenson/ICTUKIndex.html

79. Symantec: *Security Response: Hoaxes*
   www.symantec.com/avcenter/hoax.html

80. Taylor, R.P. (1980) 'Introduction', in Taylor, R.P. (ed.) *The Computer in the School: Tutor, Tool, Tutee*. New York: Teachers College Press, pages 1–10.

81. *Thinking Together*
   www.thinkingtogether.org.uk/

82. TTA: *New Opportunities Fund ICT Training Initiative for Teachers and School Librarians*
   www.tta.gov.uk/teaching/ict/nof/nof.htm

83. TTA/DfES (2002) *Qualifying to Teach: Professional Standards for Qualified Teacher Status and Requirements for Initial Teacher Training*. London: TTA.
   www.tta.gov.uk/training/qtsstandards/

84. Twining, P. *The Computer Practice Framework*
   www.med8.info/cpf/index.htm

85. Twining, P. (2003a) *dICTatED – Discussing ICT, Aspirations & Targets for Education: Interim Analysis*
   kn.open.ac.uk/public/document.cfm?documentid=2946

86. Twining, P. (2003b) *Discussing ICT, Aspirations & Targets for Education – Results Index*
   www.med8.info/qqa/results.htm

87. Underwood, J. and Brown, J. (eds) (1997) *Integrated Learning Systems: Potential into Practice*. London: Heinemann.

88. VTC: *Learning with ICT at the Foundation Stage*
   vtc.ngfl.gov.uk/docserver.php?docid=2666

89. VTC: *Teacher Resource Exchange*
   tre.ngfl.gov.uk/

90. Wegerif, R. and Scrimshaw, P. (eds) (1997) *Computers and Talk in the Primary Classroom*. Clevedon: Multilingual Matters.

91. Wood, D. (1998) *The UK ILS Evaluations – Final Report*. Coventry: BECTa.

92. Woollard, J. *Health and Safety*. University of Southampton.
   www.soton.ac.uk/~pgce/ict/hs/

93. Worcestershire LEA: *Advice on Using the Worcestershire ICT Development Planning Matrix*
    www.content.networcs.net/ngfl/ngflmatrix_pages.htm

94. *Yahooligans!*
    www.yahooligans.com/